QUEEN'S ENGLISH

QUEEN'S ENGLISH

by Vanessa Brooks

JOSEF WEINBERGER PLAYS

LONDON

QUEEN'S ENGLISH
First published in 2006
by Josef Weinberger Ltd
12-14 Mortimer Street, London, W1T 3JJ
www.josef-weinberger.com
general.info@jwmail.co.uk

Copyright © 2006 by Vanessa Brooks.
Copyright © 2005 as an unpublished dramatic composition by Vanessa Brooks.

The author asserts her moral right to be identified as the author of the work.

ISBN 0 85676 287 3

This play is protected by Copyright. According to Copyright Law, no public performance or reading of a protected play or part of that play may be given without prior authorisation from Josef Weinberger Plays, as agent for the Copyright Owners.

From time to time it is necessary to restrict or even withdraw the rights of certain plays. **It is therefore essential to check with us before making a commitment to produce a play.**

NO PERFORMANCE MAY BE GIVEN WITHOUT A LICENCE

AMATEUR PRODUCTIONS
Royalties are due at least one calendar month prior to the first performance. A royalty quotation will be issued upon receipt of the following details:

Name of Licensee
Play Title
Place of Performance
Dates and Number of Performances
Audience Capacity
Ticket Prices

PROFESSIONAL PRODUCTIONS
All enquiries regarding professional rights (other than first class rights) should be addressed to Josef Weinberger at the address above. Enquiries for all other rights should be addressed to The Narrow Road Company, 182 Brighton Road, Coulsden, Surrey CR5 2NF.

OVERSEAS PRODUCTIONS
Applications for productions overseas should be addressed to our local authorised agents. Further details are listed in our catalogue of plays, published every two years, or available from Josef Weinberger Plays at the address above.

CONDITIONS OF SALE
This book is sold subject to the condition that it shall not by way of trade or otherwise be resold, hired out, circulated or distributed without prior consent of the Publisher. **Reproduction of the text either in whole or part and by any means is strictly forbidden.**

Printed in England by Commercial Colour Press plc, Hainault, Essex

QUEEN'S ENGLISH was first produced at the Watford Palace Theatre on 3rd November 2005, with the following cast:

DAVID	Jotham Annan
JIM	Martin Ledwith
BRIDIE	Annie Farr
GEORGE	Daniel Hill
RUBY	Marilyn Cutts

Directed by Lawrence Till and Joyce Branagh
Designed by Richard Foxton

CHARACTERS

DAVID	30s. Welsh. Black. Gay. Cheerfully resigned. Optimistically suicidal.
JIM	30s / 40s. Scottish. Macho. Collector of bad taste jokes.
BRIDIE	Late 30s. Northern Irish. Spiky and weary.
GEORGE	40s. English. Divorced father. Deliriously exhausted, permanently embarrassed.
RUBY	50s / 60s. Jewish New Yorker. Business-minded, sassy and wry.
HER MAJESTY QUEEN ELIZABETH II	70s. Wealthy. Distant. Fond of things covered in fur.

TIME AND PLACE

The United School of English is based in a Grade 1 Listed country house, somewhere in the green belt to the north of London.

The action takes place in the teachers' room at the College over the course of one day, April 23rd, this year.

Thanks to:

Miriam, my best friend and critic. For her brilliance, honesty and insight – and the trip to Majdanek Concentration Camp in Poland, which inspired the chain of thought and debate which led to this play. For the endless discussions, the rigour, the big laughs – and the unreturnable forehand drive.

ACT ONE

Scene One

The teachers' room. 8.30 AM.

A grotty basement in an old country house. A series of high windows offer a view out to the grounds where a Union Jack and Stars and Stripes hang limply from an ancient flag post. Legs can be seen as they approach and leave the main entrance to the building. A communication system has evolved between the inner and outer worlds involving leaning down or stretching up and shouting.

One exit leads out to a corridor, where a Coca-Cola machine is just visible.

A St George's flag is extended over the crumbling ceiling.

Various educational and residential junk litters the room, musical instruments, plastic London souvenirs (policemen's helmets, etc), building blocks, a broken lawnmower, piping, polystyrene tiles, paint rollers and buckets.

A short ladder leans against a wall.

A large central 'table' (a flat panel on top of trestles) groans under the weight of books, papers and teaching materials. Around the edge of the room there are other tables, bookshelves, pigeon holes, notice boards, a darkened mirror, a mass-manufactured print of the Queen, a fax machine and all manner of redundant stuff that has accumulated over years of teaching. The school bell (once a servant's bell) is next to the doorway. A large whiteboard is mounted on one wall. An old non-functioning photocopier sits in one corner. Wires and tools litter the room – renovations are in progress. A free-standing microphone sits on a desk below the windows.

An antique pistol in a glass case is mounted above a bricked up Georgian fireplace.

JIM *strikes a match against the 'No Smoking' sign, lights a cigarette and leans back against a desk.* DAVID, *in striped pajamas, struggles to open the windows using a long pole.* BRIDIE *works on the broken photocopier, head in its gizzards.*

JIM	There's an Englishman, an Irishman – correction – there's an Englishman, an Irish*woman* . . .

(BRIDIE'*s head appears from inside the photocopier – she's filthy.*)

BRIDIE	Piss off, Jim. It's Monday morning.
JIM	A Scotsman and a Welshman . . .
DAVID	Recipe for disaster.

(DAVID *picks up the ladder, narrowly missing* BRIDIE'S *head as she returns to the photocopier.* DAVID *sets about fixing up a CCTV and PA system, attaching a bit to his drill and climbing the ladder.*)

JIM	So – this Englishman . . .

(GEORGE *enters and searches for his whistle on a string.*)

GEORGE	Bridie . . . Bridie . . .
BRIDIE	(*from inside the photocopier*) What?
GEORGE	Good. You're here. David. Jim. Why are there fifteen pubescent Bulgarians loitering on the driveway?
JIM	Fifteen.
GEORGE	Yes.
JIM	Pubescent.
GEORGE	Yes.

DAVID	Bulgarians.
JIM	Bulgarians.
GEORGE	Bulgarians. Yes. Why?

(*A silence.*)

GEORGE I see. Can someone give me a hand? (*Checking his watch.*) Breakfast sitting starts ... Now.

(GEORGE *rings the bell twice. It rings around the building.*)

GEORGE A hand. Please. Anybody.

(GEORGE *exits, blowing his whistle.*)

JIM So. This Englishman. This Scotsman. This Irishwoman and this Welshman – they're all flying at forty thousand feet above the North Sea.

(GEORGE'S *feet run past the open window.*)

GEORGE (*off*) Hello ... Hello ...

(GEORGE *blows his whistle.*)

JIM Suddenly a storm blows in. The engines flutter and fail. The plane plummets like a rock towards the icy waters. But the Welshman – he finds three parachutes.

DAVID No – just the three, like? And there are four of them.

BRIDIE What kind of a plane has only three parachutes?

JIM A joke plane.

DAVID You can't just stick a parachute on and jump, you know. You need training.

JIM   It's a gag.

BRIDIE   You wouldn't be able to breathe. Let alone put a harness on.

(GEORGE'S *feet appear and then his head appears at the window.*)

GEORGE   I'm waiting.

(*No reaction.*)

GEORGE   Thank you.

(GEORGE'S *head disappears again. He crunches off into the garden. The sound of a coach revving up.*)

JIM   Three parachutes. Four potential victims.

BRIDIE   David – can you hand me a screwdriver please?

(DAVID *crosses to* BRIDIE *and gives her a spanner, she dives back into the photocopier.*)

DAVID   Here you go.

JIM   Says the Welshman to the Irishwoman and he hands her a . . .

BRIDIE   Screwdriver, David. Christ.

(BRIDIE *hands the spanner back to* DAVID. *He finds a screwdriver, hands it to her and returns to his work.*)

DAVID   Sorry.

JIM   He hands her a parachute. 'You deserve to live,' he says. She puts it on and jumps out of the plane. 'Here you are,' says the Welshman to the Scotsman, buckles him up and pushes him out of the door. Finally the Welshman turns to the Englishman. He picks up the parachute and hands it over. 'Wait a minute –

	I can't expect you to make that sort of sacrifice,' says the Englishman. 'No – it's OK,' says the Welshman. 'I gave the Scotsman my rucksack.'
DAVID	Not to be trusted, our lot. All Welsh people are double-crossing sheep-shaggers. Isn't that right Bridie?
BRIDIE	Whatever.
JIM	Bang on the money, Taffy.
BRIDIE	(*kicking the photocopier*) God and all the saints.
DAVID	Where?
BRIDIE	I have had it with this.
DAVID	Had it with what?
BRIDIE	With teaching my tits off with three testosterone pumped egomaniacs for company, what do you think?
JIM	No, yer tits are still on. I can see them.
DAVID	Two testosterone pumped egomaniacs . . .
BRIDIE	God help me.
DAVID	And a pouf from Pontypridd.
JIM	I can see your pert catholic nipples straining against the fabric of your bra.
BRIDIE	My nipples are not catholic. My nipples are atheist. Godless. Stateless and unbound by the rule of international law. So back off.
JIM	Renegade baps.
DAVID	Fancy that.

BRIDIE   Christ almighty. This photocopier is knackered. Can somebody give me some . . .

JIM   David.

DAVID   Jim?

JIM   What's the difference between a woman with PMT and a pit bull terrier?

BRIDIE   Arsehole.

JIM   Lipstick.

(BRIDIE *gives* JIM *the finger.* DAVID *drills into the wall.* JIM *does nothing. A thumping is heard from above. All look up.*)

BRIDIE ⎤   OH NO – well friggin' done.
DAVID ⎦   Sorry. I'm sorry.

(JIM *apes the movements he imagines are being made in the room above.*)

JIM   She's up. She rises. She leaps from the bed. She moves the golden Passover candlesticks from under her pillow.

BRIDIE   What are you on?

JIM   Hides them in her knickers and sucks on her first pickled herring of the day.

BRIDIE   (*to* DAVID) Did you have to?

DAVID   I'm only following orders.

BRIDIE   A few more minutes free of the Cranky Yankee would have been most welcome.

(*A further thumping, all look up and trace her footsteps across the floor above with their eyes. The coach horn parps angrily outside.*)

JIM	She crosses to the window. Spies the insurrection on the drive and calls on her forefathers to curse the uncircumcised rabble below.
DAVID	Speak for yourself.
JIM	Noticing movement at the gate she gathers her prayer shawl to her and . . . (JIM *picks up a decorator's cloth and wraps it round himself.*)
BRIDIE	That's men, you ignoramus. Men wear prayer shawls.
JIM	And invoking the names of Moses and Mohammed . . .
BRIDIE	That's Islam.
JIM	She plans a Jewish revenge for the British gentiles.
BRIDIE	It's like Bernard Manning with verbal diarrhoea.
JIM	A Scotsman. An Irish*woman* . . .
DAVID	You've got him going now.
JIM	. . . and a Jewish woman are lost in the dessert. Weak desperate and dying.
BRIDIE	Why can't these freaks just eat lunch. Or read the paper. Why is it always life and death? Friggin pot-holes and glaciers.
JIM	Ups the ante – makes it funny.
BRIDIE	You sure about that?

JIM   The Scotsman says I'm tired and I'm thirsty I must have a wee dram. The Irishwoman says I'm tired and I'm thirsty I must have a Guinness.

BRIDIE   Hate the stuff.

JIM   The Jewish woman says. I'm tired and I'm thirsty I must have diabetes . . . Gotcha. You're smiling. Isn't she, David? Isn't she smiling?

DAVID   Hard to tell. Might be indigestion.

JIM   If you get it. You know it. You've bought in, sweetie.

BRIDIE   You're such a coward. You don't say this stuff to her face.

JIM   Me – a coward? I say it like it is. Stand my ground. No one censors me.

BRIDIE   Change the record.

JIM   Lie down with the English long enough you end up with milk for blood.

BRIDIE   Lie down with the Scottish you end up with thistles up your arse. And they make you pay to pull them out.

JIM   We rule ourselves, lassie. We've an assembly.

BRIDIE   You've an overpriced office block stuffed with overpaid beaurocrats. Puppets. Bloody puppets. London pulls your strings.

JIM   You could do far worse than a Scot, sweetie. Aye. That's for sure.

BRIDIE   In your dreams.

JIM	Nightmare for me, babe. This haggis needs slow cooking in a quality oven.
DAVID	Don't look at me. As far as you're concerned I'm vegetarian.
JIM	I'm not looking at you. I never look at you.
DAVID	That why you keep bumping into me, is it?
JIM	What? What are you . . .

(GEORGE *enters, a parcel under his arm, flustered. He searches for papers.*)

GEORGE	David. David. (*To* DAVID, *passing him the parcel.*) For you. Recorded. One pound ten fine and excess. I paid it but in future . . .
DAVID	(*placing the parcel on his desk*) Yes. Perfect timing.
GEORGE	Where are the accommodation lists? Please? Anyone? Brigitte Krasa wants to see them.
DAVID	Who?
JIM	She's a returnee. Residential last year with a group from Sofya.
GEORGE	What the hell did you say to her Jim? She's ready to walk. With her group. That's over five grand in fees. Lists? Anyone? Help me. What did you say? What did you say to her?
JIM	Nothing. I was having a laugh.
GEORGE	Bridie. Have you seen the . . .

(BRIDIE *turns her back on* GEORGE.)

JIM	I didn't expect her to get it.
BRIDIE	Then why say it?

DAVID	I remember Brigitte Krasa. She existed the whole of last summer on a diet of steroids and weight lifting.
GEORGE	She's training for 2012. She has an Olympic dream.
JIM	She gives me Olympic nightmares. Everybody's so quick to get their backs up.
BRIDIE	Ask yourself why.
JIM	Christ. Thought police everywhere.
GEORGE	That reminds me. The Spanish boy.
JIM	Jesus?
GEORGE	(*correcting his pronunciation*) 'H'esus. Yes. Where are they? This is absurd.
JIM	The huge great hairy lummox with the goggly eyes?
GEORGE	Last night he went for a sleepwalk and sprinkled his holy water all over the library. He's denying it and his ADHD has kicked in. He's all fists and spittle. I can't . . . I just can't . . . can't deal with it right now.
JIM	Why? Has the Princess of Egypt had your balls for a salt beef sandwich?
	(*A silence.*)
JIM	What? Can nobody take any jokes anymore?
GEORGE	Give him a bucket and some disinfectant – and be careful with the rug. It's priceless. The last Czarina of Russia gave birth on it after a hunting trip with the eighth Earl.
JIM	And there was me thinking it was a paisley pattern.

GEORGE	And Jim, I'll apologise to Brigitte Krasa. I'll apologise for you.
JIM	Cheers, George. You're a brick.
GEORGE	But you need to tell me. The joke.

(*All look at* JIM.)

JIM	Ach – it was spontaneous. It won't . . . alright. What's the difference between the Bulgarian women's track team . . .
BRIDIE ⎤ DAVID ⎦	Oh God. Here we go.
JIM	. . . and a pygmy team? The pygmies are a team of cunning runts . . . do you not see . . . So the Bulgarians are a team of . . .
GEORGE	Yes. Yes. I see. Thank you.
BRIDIE	You go too far, you eejit.
JIM	I feel a spot of wee-wee cleaning coming on.

(JIM *exits.*)

GEORGE	Where are these bloody lists? Please. Not today. I had two hours sleep. The boy he's . . . Just not today. Not with . . . her upstairs . . . She's not . . . not pleased . . . It's beyond a . . .

(BRIDIE *studiously ignores* GEORGE *whilst taking the lists from the photocopier plate and placing them on the desk in front of him.* GEORGE *can't take his eyes off* BRIDIE.)

GEORGE	Thanks. Thank you very much. Very much indeed. Bridie, I . . .
DAVID	Funny buggers, young learners, aren't they?
GEORGE	What?

DAVID	Fine in their own country but two weeks in a stately pile in Hertfordshire renders them incontinent.
GEORGE	(*distracted by* BRIDIE) Why are you still in your pyjamas?
DAVID	Must be culture shock. The horror of Wayne Rooney's IQ, Charlotte Church's sex life and the belly-pierced, shopping addicted, monosyllabic hordes guarantee there's not a dry European arse in the house.
GEORGE	It's nearly nine . . .
DAVID	From Benelux to the Basque, Europe's future pisses itself at the prospect of further integration.

(BRIDIE *bashes the photocopier.*)

GEORGE	Bridie?
DAVID	They should hand out rubber pants at Dover.
GEORGE	What? David. Clothes. Please.
DAVID	I've not had a moment, George. The Scandinavians kicked off before breakfast. Some smartarse whispered CJD to them and they subjected the kitchen staff to a Viking inquisition.
GEORGE	What did you say to them?
DAVID	I avoided the issue loquaciously with a circuitous gobful of advanced vocabulary. They agreed to eat their sausages. If they die it won't be of ignorance. Just incomprehension.

(BRIDIE *bashes the photocopier again.*)

GEORGE	What? (*To* BRIDIE.) I . . . I . . . I said leave it. So . . . leave it. Please.

DAVID	Then the group of Japanese learners wanted directions to PC World. Their mini-translators were water-logged on their pub night in town yesterday. A gang of psychotic binge-drinkers pushed them into the municipal fountains.
GEORGE	What?
DAVID	So I guided them from the end of the drive and made sure they had a little map for the way back. Told them to buy personal attack alarms while they were at it. For the next time they fancied an English pint.

(BRIDIE *fiddles with the machine once more, then finds an ancient iron which is being used as a doorstop.*)

GEORGE	A map. Right. Good. Yes. (*To* BRIDIE.) Please stop, Bridie. You'll make things worse.
DAVID	Our new lady owner wants me to finish wiring the CCTV and the PA and what with planning my classes, clearing the gutters, unblocking two hand basins, dishing out disco tickets and grappling at length and with febrile intensity the fundamental existential questions which have plagued poets and philosophers for centuries I've not had a moment to slip into my Farrahs and pop on my Hush Puppies.

(BRIDIE *swings the iron into a panel of the copier in a vain attempt to open it.*)

GEORGE	NO. I SAID NO. NOW LEAVE IT. NOW BLOODY LEAVE IT YOU BLOODY PIG-HEADED BLOODY STUPID BLOODY FRIGID BLOODY FEMINIST BLOODY IRISH COW.
BRIDIE	I am not frigid.
GEORGE	Ah . . . that isn't . . . that isn't what I meant to say. I didn't mean . . . In no way would I . . . I'm so sorry. Stress. A demanding child. Traffic.

Paperwork. America. And haemorrhoids. Sorry. Truly. Bridie – SHIT.

(BRIDIE *crosses to her chair and sits at her desk. She plans a class.*)

GEORGE How did you . . . how did you get on? Get on at the doctors, David?

DAVID Not great.

GEORGE Good.

DAVID Pretty awful in fact.

GEORGE Excellent.

DAVID I'm expecting a call about the – this morning. A moment of your time would be . . .

(GEORGE *musters his courage and crosses to* BRIDIE. *He eyes her teaching materials. He coughs.* BRIDIE *doesn't look up.*)

GEORGE Past simple versus continuous.

BRIDIE Are you talking to me?

GEORGE This is for your pre-intermediate class?

BRIDIE No. I'm cutting out the pretty pictures as a therapy for my frigidity. It's either that or electric shocks.

GEORGE Bridie. Please. Let's be professional, yes? (*Indicating* DAVID.) What have you planned?

BRIDIE I've been teaching for twelve sodding years. I've planned nothing.

GEORGE I'd like to see your lesson plan.

(BRIDIE *lifts her top to show* GEORGE *her bra. He covers his eyes and turns away.*)

GEORGE	STOP IT. Stop it. I am the Director of Studies. I am your boss and I am asking you to talk me through your lesson plan.
BRIDIE	Question forms. For example. What did you do last night? I waited inside a dump of a wine bar just off the High Street. Past simple. How long were you waiting? Past continuous. Pronoun plus auxiliary verb plus 'ing' form. I was waiting for an hour and a bloody half – idiomatic slang. The English wimp didn't show up. Negative past plus phrasal verb. So I decided to dump him. Past simple to indicate completed action – infinitive to explain future intention. Future is now. It's over. Finished. Final. I have had it with you. Professional enough for you?
GEORGE	I can explain.
BRIDIE	No you can't. You can disappoint. You can upset and you can destroy but you can never ever explain.
GEORGE	Bridie, I...
RUBY	(*off*) GEORGE – GEORGE – WHERE IN THE HELL ARE YA?

(JIM *appears from outside in the window.*)

JIM	GEORGE (*Shouting Up.*) HE'S ON HIS WAY (*To* GEORGE.) Hurry up, man. She's dangling out of her window with a face that'd part the Red Sea.

(JIM *disappears.*)

RUBY	(*off*) DO YA HEAR ME GEORGE? – GET YOUR ARSE OUT HERE, YA CHINLESS WUSS – MOVE IT!
BRIDIE	Run along. Your mammie's calling.

(GEORGE *crosses to the window and shouts upwards.*)

GEORGE YES. YES. I'M COMING, RUBY. I'M COMING. (*To* DAVID.) Get some clothes on David. Please.

(GEORGE *exits.* BRIDIE *slumps at her desk.*)

(*A silence.*)

BRIDIE Come 'ere.

(DAVID *slowly downs tools and walks to* BRIDIE.)

BRIDIE Closer. Bend over.

(DAVID *bends over.* BRIDIE *take a cigarette from* DAVID'S *top pocket, followed by a lighter, she lights up.* GEORGE'S *legs can be seen crunching past the window.*)

GEORGE (*off*) HELLO – I SAY HELLO ...

DAVID Oh – You were doing so well, too.

BRIDIE One month on. One month off. I figure when I do get the big C it'll just be in the one lung.

(*A silence.*)

(DAVID *returns to his work, stopping to touch his parcel.* BRIDIE *watches him.*)

BRIDIE Not your birthday, is it?

DAVID No.

BRIDIE Good. 'Cos no one's got you anything.

(*A silence.*)

(DAVID *continues fixing up the CCTV.* BRIDIE *crosses to pick up a dictionary and spots her dirt-smeared face in the mirror.*)

BRIDIE	Oh my God. Why didn't you tell me?
DAVID	I thought you'd shout at me.
BRIDIE	Brilliant. I look like Pocohontas. No wonder he doesn't take me seriously.

(BRIDIE *cleans up her face and sits back at her desk. She tries to work but ultimately screws up the piece of paper.*)

DAVID	It's not easy for George. Single father.
BRIDIE	Only two days a week.
DAVID	Responsibilities.
BRIDIE	Not easy being a single bloody woman. No one every considers that, do they?
DAVID ⎤ BRIDIE ⎦	Yes. Drop it. I've got twelve original drawings of a cockless male body to do since we've got no mechanical back-up.
DAVID	Maybe I can help.
BRIDIE	Modelling?
DAVID	Listening. You can bend my ear if you want to – I . . .
BRIDIE ⎤ DAVID ⎦	Oh spare me the sympathy of friggin' Wales. Not a colleague thing . . . a friend thing.
BRIDIE	Friends? I don't need any more friends. I've got friends coming out of my ears. Gay friends. Christ.
DAVID	What?

(BRIDIE *expertly gathers various materials and books from around the room occasionally making notes, on auto-pilot.*)

BRIDIE	I don't want to be a mother figure for you. I don't want to watch your pornography with you or tell you your arse looks good in white jeans. I don't want to sit grinning like a sexless Madonna in rooms full of men eyeing each other up. I'm a woman, David. A woman. Do you understand that? Do you?
DAVID	Yes.
BRIDIE	Careering towards forty. Do you understand that?
DAVID	Yes.
BRIDIE	Forty.
DAVID	Forty. Yes. I understand that.
BRIDIE	I don't want to waste a moment of my time with an action man with a chiselled chin and rigor mortis in his pants.
DAVID	No. That would be insane.
BRIDIE	Jesus, what is it with you guys? You say you don't like women but you want the whole shebang without giving anything back. What do you want to spend time with us for?
DAVID	Search me.
BRIDIE	I'll tell you why . . .
DAVID	Okay.
BRIDIE	So that we can endlessly give and give and give and make you feel better about yourselves doling out the ready acceptance that your mothers and sisters can't provide well enough is enough sod you and making you feel better I want to feel good about me. I want a man. A red blooded passionate sweaty muscle and gristle coated lump of masculinity

	who is interested in me because I am a woman. I do not want you. Is that clear?
DAVID	Any clearer we'd share the same brain. Clear as day. Clear as a funeral bell ringing out into an empty dew-soaked valley.
BRIDIE	There's no need to go on and on and on. That's another thing your bloody lot does. Oh forget it . . . (*Puzzling over a piece of paper.*) Date. What's the date today?

(DAVID *crosses to the wall calendar.*)

DAVID	It's the 23rd of April. On this day in 1992 MacDonald's opened in China. William Shakespeare was born and it's National Peppercorn Day in Bermuda.
BRIDIE	Feels like a grind to me.
DAVID	Oh. And it's St George's Day.
BRIDIE	Bollocks to that and all.
DAVID	And on this day in 1984 . . .
BRIDIE	Shut up, David.
DAVID	It's really quite . . .
BRIDIE	I DON'T WANT TO KNOW.
DAVID	Of course you don't. Sorry.

(JIM *appears in the window.*)

JIM	The eagle is landing. And her claws are out.
BRIDIE ⎤ DAVID ⎥ JIM ⎦	Oh bloody hell. What. Now? Get all that shite off the table. Hide the ashtray.
GEORGE	(*from a distance*) JIM . . . JIM . . .

DAVID	She'll smell it anyway.
BRIDIE	(*finding perfume in bag*) No she won't. Here we go. Close your mouth. And your eyes. And stop breathing.
DAVID	Your wish is my command.

(DAVID *does so,* BRIDIE *finds perfume in her bag and sprays it liberally around the room. She nudges* DAVID.)

BRIDIE	Quick. Quickly.

(GEORGE'S *legs approach and appear next to* JIM'S. *They both disappear as they make their way into the house.* BRIDIE *clears some of the mess from the central table.* DAVID *puts chairs into correct places and makes an effort to clear a few surfaces.*)

BRIDIE	Move. Hurry up.

(JIM *enters carrying accommodation lists and rings the bell three times.*)

JIM	No. No way. You tell her. (*Clarifying bell to* BRIDIE *and* DAVID.) Pupils to classrooms. They registered ten students. It's in black and white.

(GEORGE *enters hot on* JIM'S *tails and rings the bell three times again.*)

GEORGE	(*declaiming to the room*) Pupils to classrooms.
JIM	I just did that.
GEORGE	Well don't. It's my job. It reeks in here.
JIM	We've only got ten beds for them.
GEORGE	She won't budge thanks to . . . Special needs, she says. Extra ventilation. For the one with asthma.

JIM	Asthma? Everyone's got asthma. It's not a special need, it's a stage of development.
DAVID BRIDIE GEORGE	Use the bunk beds in the stable block. It's their responsibility. Not ours. She wants to talk to you. I'm sorry Jim. I tried but you're going to have to . . .

(RUBY *enters in her dressing gown. She ignores the throng and breezes glamorously to the window. She picks up the microphone and turns it on.*)

RUBY (*amplified through the PA system*) Hold it right there, boys and girls. This is your principal Ruby Rosenberg speaking. Miss Krasa – do not board the bus. I repeat. Stay right where you are. Attagirl. Now drop da bags. I repeat, drop the bags. Good. Here is the deal. I'm gonna give ya not one day – not two days – not three days, but a whole week's free tuition – do the math – it's a deal and a half. Way to go. Can you move away from the coach? Okay – listen up. I'm gonna throw in a trip to the London Eye – hey, I'll even get them to speed it up for ya and throw in the cotton candy – I'll give ya two hours sightseeing on an open-topped bus – and – stay with me honey, it gets better – any – I repeat, any – Andrew Lloyd Webber matinee of your choosing – NO NO COME BACK GET OFF THE COACH GET BACK INTO LINE – PLUS – a big plus – for each and every member of your group a souvenir statuette of Prince William in water polo trunks. Royal quality schmutter in the hand, no questions asked. And as for little Jan – dear adorable little Jan with the watery eyes and the wheezy chest and the wet little schnoz – he will be accommodated in the King's dressing room and provided with a state-of-the-art anti-allergy system dust-mite repellent and peanut sensor. Our director George will see to it that all of his dietary

	detoxification and air purification needs are met in conflab with you every morning at seven …
GEORGE	I can't start at seven.
RUBY	And again every evening at ten.
GEORGE	NO.
RUBY	Please wave to agree the deal. I'm assumin' you say yes with two fingers in Bulgaria, Ms Krasa. Everyone away and off the coach now. Attagirl. And the cross-eyed kid on the back seat with the flick knife. And the bald kid with his hands round the driver's neck. Terrific. Class starts in ten minutes. In the meantime please sample the new double chocolate cream doughnuts and frappucinos being trailed from the hatch in the Olde English Refectory. On the house. Love, respect, peace and harmony to you Ms Krasa. You are a wise and wonderful woman.

(RUBY *turns off the PA in a surge of feedback.*)

RUBY	Any bullshit, send the muscle-brained transvestite to me. So what's the story? Who crapped on the strawberries and pissed on my parade?

(*A silence.*)

RUBY	Some schmuck rocked the Bulgarian boat – who was it?
GEORGE	I … (*Lying to save* JIM.) It was me.
RUBY	Well what'd ya know. What in God's name is that stink? The United Kingdom is an assault to the senses. Saturated fat. BO and cheap perfume.
BRIDIE	Not that cheap. It's 'Poison'.

JIM	That's for sure.
RUBY	Has some deadhead been smoking in here? Only Neanderthals and Frenchmen smoke. I thought you lot were a stage further on in your evolution. Unhygienic. It's all so old and dirty. I'm gonna get the industrial cleaners in. Rip up the floor.
GEORGE	What?
RUBY	Get this old paper off the walls.

(RUBY *grabs at the wallpaper.*)

GEORGE	STOP. That's William Morris. This is a listed building.
RUBY	Listed schmisted. We need colour. Lights. Technology. Showers. How do you get clean sitting in your own dirty bathwater? Heating, for Christ's sake.
GEORGE	There's no need to turn ourselves into a theme park.
RUBY	Oh yes there is. You ain't seen the books.
BRIDIE DAVID JIM GEORGE	Can't we close while we do the building work it... There are implications with the heritage people, I... My classroom is choked up with dust as it is... You simply can't vandalise a great....
RUBY	SHUT UP the lot of yous. Sit down and listen. I got an announcement to make. SIT.

(*All sit.* GEORGE *finally, reluctantly at the end of* RUBY'S *stare.*)

RUBY	This afternoon we are going to have ourselves a grand re-opening.
JIM	I didn't know we'd closed.

GEORGE Our previous owner would never have allowed . . .

RUBY You've been taken over, buddy boy, and don't you forget it. The Earl lost this place fair and square in a poker game. He and I spat and shook hands on Mustique. The lease is mine. Deal with it. Now. You've got a new menu. New drinks machine. An integrated security and surveillance system. Computers. Soon you get a new syllabus.

GEORGE What? You can't change . . .

BRIDIE That's more work. We can't . . .

RUBY This ain't a meeting, it's an announcement. I been working on something. For months. Took all my schmoozing skills and cost a packet in sweeteners. But I got the prize. Boy did I get the prize. I have lined up a class act. The classiest act to cut the ribbon this afternoon. Now. Name me a great British figure who represents you all.

(*A silence.*)

GEORGE Jeremy Clarkson.

JIM Sean Connery.

DAVID Catherine Zeta Jones.

BRIDIE Gloria Hunniford.

RUBY Close but no cigar. At two thirty this afternoon we shall be receiving the Queen.

BRIDIE Graham Norton?

RUBY The Monarch. Not any old Joe Schmoe but Her Majesty, the triumphant Head of the Commonwealth herself. The most noble, sacred, gracious sovereign of all sparkling and twinkling and looking a million bucks will be

	here today in all her glory. The Queen is coming.
GEORGE	I'm sorry . . . *The* Queen.
RUBY	The real McCoy.
GEORGE	Are you sure?
RUBY	I may be a dumb broad from the Bronx but they ain't gonna dupe me on this one. The genuine corgi-toting tiara wearing blue-blooded highness dame is gonna be glove-handedly squeezin' ya mits this afternoon. What do you say to that?
GEORGE	I'm not sure we're equipped.
JIM	I'm nae bothered. She's their Queen, not mine.
BRIDIE	Suppose she needs to pee?
GEORGE	What? The Queen doesn't pee.
BRIDIE	I've been pissing in the sink in the gardener's shed. The staff ladies' is buggered. I don't suppose . . .
RUBY	All arranged. She gets the call she can use mine. Don't have a cow if you see a few secret service guys checking the . . .
GEORGE	Just a minute . . . just a . . . Her diary is booked up for months. Years.
RUBY	I told ya. I been working on it. When *I* work stuff happens.
GEORGE	Why was I not informed earlier?
RUBY	Security reasons.
GEORGE	How bloody convenient.

RUBY	The helicopter will land on the rose garden at . . .
GEORGE	No. NO. Sorry. Putting my foot down. That's Capability Brown landscaping.
RUBY	Capability Ruby's now. Besides. I think being divinely appointed by God gives you the right to muzz up a few rose bushes, don't you? God beats greenfly every time.
GEORGE	I . . . I . . .
RUBY	Let's shift ass. Go tell your students.
GEORGE	What? What? Wait, I . . .

(RUBY *rings the school bell three times.*)

RUBY	You get a full briefing later.
GEORGE	It's four rings. Four rings for lesson one.

(GEORGE *rings the bell four times. Everyone makes ready to go into their classrooms.*)

RUBY	I want quite a show laid on for Lizzie – this is the beginning of great things for us. Move it. Class time. Go lick 'em into shape with your big fat mother tongues.
GEORGE	For pity's sake.
JIM	Is she gonna like – talk to us? Talk to me? One to one like?
RUBY	(*pushing* JIM *out of the door*) There'll be a lot of waving and nodding but actual verbals I ain't so sure. Now shoot.

(JIM *exits.*)

BRIDIE	This has been worked out properly? There will be a schedule?

RUBY	Untwist your pantyhose, missy all will be revealed.
BRIDIE	Don't leave the planning to George. We'll all end up in the tower.
GEORGE	You ...

(BRIDIE *exits.*)

RUBY	(*to* DAVID) I put your kids in with Bridie's. Go knock yourself out with a whipped cream frappuccino.
DAVID	Rightie ho.
RUBY	It's the business.

(DAVID *exits.* GEORGE *picks up his books and papers and makes to follow* DAVID.)

GEORGE	It gives the wrong impression Ruby. Coffee and doughnuts. This is an English School. The British Empire was built on scones, cucumber sandwiches and rich tea biscuits.
RUBY	So that's why it crumbled. Hold it right there, buster.

(RUBY *closes the door in front of* GEORGE.)

RUBY	Park your ass. We gotta talk. On the QT.

(GEORGE *sits checking his watch.*)

GEORGE	Class has started.
RUBY	You got it on with Bridie yet? That dame needs some stress relief.
GEORGE	I beg your pardon?

RUBY Loosen up George. This is a residential college. You fart in the west wing I smell it on the croquet lawn.

GEORGE That's not how it works here.

RUBY You don't fart?

GEORGE We don't sniff. It's the British way.

RUBY It still stinks.

GEORGE Good. Well. Now we've got that straight I'll get on with my job.

(GEORGE *heads towards the door.*)

RUBY This house. It's what – two – three hundred years old?

GEORGE It's regency actually.

RUBY How many years is that?

GEORGE Queen Charlotte – the wife of George the third . . .

RUBY The one who went loop-di-doo?

GEORGE Not the technical term.

RUBY I saw the movie. Great toupes. Too much shit.

GEORGE She stayed here. Queen Charlotte. On her way to the coast. In your bedroom. In fact.

RUBY No way. I'm sleeping where a Queen slept? If I rub the four poster hard enough will some of her DNA mix with my DNA and make me special?

GEORGE Probably not. No. That flag post out there is made from one of the masts on Nelson's ship at the battle of Trafalgar.

RUBY	Didn't he miss it?

(GEORGE *crosses to the gun in its case.*)

GEORGE	And this gun. This gun, Ruby, started the first world war. This gun shaped the modern world. This gun changed everything. Forever.
RUBY	How come?
GEORGE	Gavrilo Princip took aim with this gun and assassinated the Archduke Ferdinand in Sarajevo. His treason rocked a nation. Destabilised a region and sparked the bloodiest war in modern history. One man. One gun. One shot. That's all it took . . . It's extremely valuable.
RUBY	Just like the picture of the crazy horse with the fat neck?
GEORGE	The Stubbs. Yes.

(RUBY *finds piece of paper in her pocket and reads.*)

RUBY	There's a photo here. In the Earl's inventory for the house. Plus a fourteenth century suit of armour. Priceless pewter-ware. Various collectables from the Arts and Crafts movement and a jousting pole.
GEORGE	Priceless. Yes.
RUBY	So where is it? Where's it all gone George? I go to the attic. Nothing. I go to the cellars. Nada. Now I got a problem. Everything's picture perfect. The staff. The location. Hell, Her Majesty is going to give us the kind of publicity money can't buy, but . . . I need the gear, George. I need to sell the past to pay for the future.

GEORGE | I . . . I . . . It was all . . . all here last week. I . . . You think someone's . . . that someone's . . .

RUBY | Let's not involve the cops. Not yet. All I want is a name. Anyone been acting kooky recently?

(DAVID *enters with styrofoam cup.*)

DAVID | There's a man in a black suit with dark glasses on in reception. Says he's Royal protection.

RUBY | (*to* GEORGE) A name. Understood?

(RUBY *exits.*)

DAVID | George I need to talk to you. It's important. Please.

GEORGE | Shh.

(GEORGE *approaches the CCTV camera and inspects it.*)

GEORGE | She's watching us.

DAVID | No she's not. She can't be. I checked the circuit. It's the same as the lights. Dead. (*Snapping the light switch on and off – no change.*) She's waiting on an electrician – could be weeks. We're friends, aren't we George? You and me? I just need to . . .

GEORGE | Take some time off. Tomorrow.

DAVID | Five minutes. That's all I need.

RUBY | (*on PA*) SHIFT YOUR BUTT GEORGE. You got a gaggle of Iranians doin' formulae on the white board in the drawing room. Go teach 'em something before they go nuclear.

DAVID | She's rigged up a mike in reception. But she can't see you.

RUBY	(*on PA*) Now.
GEORGE	Coming.
	(GEORGE *exits.*)
DAVID	But I need to . . .
	(DAVID's *mobile rings. He takes it out of his pocket.*)
DAVID	Hello . . . Yes. That's me . . . Just a moment . . .
	(DAVID *sits, ready for bad news.*)
DAVID	Go ahead.
	(*Blackout.*)

Scene Two

The same. 10:00 AM. JIM *is admiring himself in the mirror.*

JIM	Jim MacMillan. Call me Jim, your Majesty. Jim. I teach. I lead. They follow. Six foot two. Fourteen stone. Strength of an ox.
	(GEORGE *enters unnoticed carrying a sports bag.*)
JIM	The looks of Ewan McGregor and the wit of Billy Connolly. I am your humble servant, your Majesty.
GEORGE	Jim?
JIM	Though I oppose completely and utterly your opposition to a free Scotland. And bollocks to dictatorship from England. Didn't see you there.
	(JIM *returns to his desk.*)

GEORGE   No. I snook up in my sneakers. Nobody wears shoes with proper soles anymore. Have you noticed that? Everyone's being muffled. (*Laying out his cricket gear.*) God bless America. They've given us Britney Spears, sodium dependency and the ability to sneak up on each other from behind.

JIM   Could have been worse. The new boss could have been German.

GEORGE   Shouldn't you be . . . well . . . you know. Teaching. (*Checking timetable on wall.*) In 4A?

JIM   Left them to it. Japanese. Wind them up. Off they go. Eyes down pens up. Like clockwork beetles.

GEORGE   Asian diligence. Yes. Should be bottled and drip fed to the Latins.

JIM   What do you call it when an Italian has one arm shorter than the other?

GEORGE   I don't know.

JIM   A speech impediment.

(GEORGE *raises his eyebrows dully and changes into cricket gear.* JIM *turns back to his work.*)

GEORGE   I took the boy for a pair of trousers yesterday.

JIM   Oh Aye?

GEORGE   He ended up with a pair of mine cut off. Eight years old and he's got a beer belly. I don't understand it. I feed him enough organic vegetables to make him jet-propelled. Ruby says it's the terrorists. They're putting something in sherbet fountains. Making the

	kids so bloody fat they won't be able to get their fingers round a trigger.
JIM	What's the name of the new face cream specially developed for Jewish women?
GEORGE	Jim.
JIM	Oil of 'Oi Vey.' Get it? Oil of . . .
GEORGE	I've saved you twice today and it's not even lunchtime.
JIM	Give me a break. Bulgarian wine – delicious. Bulgarian music – moody. But the Bulgarian sense of humour? I raised more laughs from my depressive Uncle Angus. And that was after he'd choked to death.
GEORGE	Yes, but . . .

(JIM *searches in his desk for materials.*)

JIM	I like to know what people are thinking, George. Good or bad. I don't want it buried. Neither should you. Got to be able to laugh at ourselves.
GEORGE	At ourselves, yes, not at . . .
JIM	You should get out more. You look like shite.
GEORGE	Thank you.
JIM	The lads are meeting tonight. Come along. Few jars. Good crack.
GEORGE	Survivalism isn't really my thing, Jim. I've got sensitive skin. One sniff of a bramble and I come out in hives. Besides I'm on nursemaid duty. Didn't you hear?

JIM	We've moved on. It's combat now. Armed and unarmed. Can I take those fencing swords again?
GEORGE	What?
JIM	Have 'em back first thing.
GEORGE	No. No, you can't.
JIM	What are you talking about? I had the mace and those shields last week. We recreated Bannockburn in the multi storey car park.
GEORGE	It's not a good time. To be borrowing things.
JIM	I promised the guys. WHY?
GEORGE	Oh God.
	(GEORGE *closes the door.*)
GEORGE	(*whispering*) It's Ruby.
	(GEORGE *looks up into the CCTV camera anxiously.*)
JIM	What?
GEORGE	It's Ruby she's . . .
JIM	SPEAK UP, MAN.
GEORGE	Ruby is gunning for someone. She wants a head on a platter. One of us is for the chop. The big heave-ho. The push.
	(JIM *springs to his feet, suddenly panicked.*)
JIM	No. NO. NO I cannae lose my job. I cannae lose my job. I cannae, do you hear me?
GEORGE	Jim. Listen, I . . .

JIM	I'll never get another one. You know that. I thought we were safe. You said we were safe. You said we were all safe.
GEORGE	No one's safe anymore. Anywhere.
JIM	You stand up to her for once. TELL HER NO.
GEORGE	Keep your voice down for . . .
JIM	No way. Jesus, I knew it. I knew it. The Yiddisher mamma stuff is an act. It's a Jewish thing I'm telling you. Smiling, but underneath the sheitel it's all counting out the shekels in the tent.
GEORGE	Sheitel? Tent? Shekels?
JIM	Money-grabbing tight-fistedness.
GEORGE	I thought that was the Scots.
JIM	There's no changing it. It's just who we are. Like I'm a warrior like you're spineless and like Bridies an alcoholic.
GEORGE	A what? No, she . . .
JIM	You tell her. Tell her you're standing by me. Tell her if I go we all go. GEORGE. DO YOU HEAR ME MAN? I'M NOT KIDDING.
GEORGE	You're not listening to . . .
JIM	I CANNOT LOSE MY JOB. YOU HEAR ME? BE LOYAL FOR ONCE.
	(JIM *grabs* GEORGE *by collar and holds him against the wall.*)
GEORGE	IT'S . . . NOT . . . YOU.
JIM	Eh?

GEORGE	Let go of me, Jim. Please. Let go. There's a good chap.

(JIM *lets go.* GEORGE *gasps for breath.*)

GEORGE	Is that what they call a Glasgow kiss?
JIM	No that's a head butt.
GEORGE	Right.
JIM	That was an Edinburgh hug.
GEORGE	Very warm. Yes.

(JIM *slumps into chair, it dawns on him that he's flown off the handle.*)

JIM	(*laughing*) You had me there, George. You had me there.
GEORGE	(*rubbing his neck*) No. You had me, Jim. You had me.
JIM	I saw my whole life flash before me. My credit card bills are thicker than the phone directory. Bloody hell.
GEORGE	It's not a cost-cutting exercise. She thinks someone is . . . up to something. She doesn't know who. She wants me to find out.
JIM	What? You're telling me there's a traitor. A traitor in our midst.
GEORGE	Not quite so medieval. A thief, Jim. Objects are missing from the house. A thief.
JIM	Same difference.
GEORGE	Is it?
JIM	Screws us all over. Christ. We don't need this.

GEORGE	Just don't be seen touching anything. Just be . . . on your guard. Don't worry. I'll sort it all out. Could you give me a hand?
	(GEORGE *tries to fix a pad to his leg.* JIM *doesn't move.*)
JIM	I know who it is.
GEORGE	There's something about putting whites on.
JIM	It all makes sense now. I mean we three it's all for one and one for all. But with him. Well he's different, isn't he? He just is . . . different. You know. George. George. Don't you agree?
GEORGE	Always equated cricket kit with decency. Fair play. Gentlemanly behaviour, eh Jim?
JIM	He's Welsh, for starters.
GEORGE	Pass me that tie would you? Hoping we can show the Queen our little Belgian Bowler. Have you seen his googlies?
	(JIM *hands* GEORGE *a tie which* GEORGE *uses as a belt as he looks out of the window.*)
JIM	I've often wondered . . . .
GEORGE	Lovely day out there. Perfect. She'll see us at our best.
JIM	George, stop the avoidance crap – listen to me . . . Often thought – David – he might be . . . I mean he could be . . . a Muslim.
GEORGE	What?
JIM	A lot of blacks are Muslims.
GEORGE	So are a lot of whites, pinks, yellows and every hue in between. Pass me my jumper please.

JIM: It's a possibility. That's all. He could be a Muslim.

(JIM *passes* GEORGE *his jumper.* GEORGE *puts it on, puzzled.*)

GEORGE: No he couldn't. He isn't. You know he isn't. He was brought up chapel, he eats fish fingers on Fridays and he knows all the words to 'Morning Has Broken'.

JIM: Could be operating under deep cover.

GEORGE: Operating? The only thing David can operate is nose clippers. And what's being Muslim got to do with . . .

JIM: Hear me out. And he's black, you see. I'm sorry, George but it has to be said. He is black.

GEORGE: So is Moira Stuart.

JIM: Ah, but Moira Stuart doesn't take it up the Khyber Pass.

GEORGE: What? What the hell are you driving at?

JIM: Steady.

GEORGE: Don't steady me. I don't like . . . (*Speaking more quietly.*) I don't like where this is headed, Jim.

JIM: I'm just saying. He's got plenty of reason to bear a grudge. Outsider, isn't he? Hell, I'd have a chip on my shoulder. He's never really fitted in.

GEORGE: Not everybody arm wrestles and tells filthy jokes.

JIM: And he likes Girls Aloud.

GEORGE: So do I.

JIM	You're just sex-starved. He's twisted.
GEORGE	This is bigoted nonsense.
JIM	It's a truth. You can try. Aye we all try. But you cannae fully trust any of them, George.

(GEORGE *is suddenly furious.*)

GEORGE	WELSHMEN, HOMOSEXUALS OR MUSLIMS?
JIM	You said it.
GEORGE	I DID NOT BLOODY SAY IT. YOU DID.
JIM	I love the guy, George. Love him. But I don't trust him. He's got a different agenda. Must have. Think about it. It's got to be one of us, right?
GEORGE	Yes. No. Could be other staff – unlikely, but . . .
JIM	So face it. If he's guilty, he's guilty. Makes no odds what ilk he is.
GEORGE	Then why have you done nothing but talk about ilk for the last five minutes? Enough. Subject closed. Understood? I am not having this conversation. On this day of all days. What's happened to you? Something's changed.
JIM	Times change.
GEORGE	Decency doesn't. Not cricket, Jim. Just not cricket.

(GEORGE *gathers his teaching clothes together and puts them back in the bag, turning his back on* JIM. BRIDIE *enters with a sheaf of papers.*)

BRIDIE	Oi – William Wallace – What's going on in your classroom?

JIM	It's called student-centred learning sweetie. Teaching them to be more autonomous.
BRIDIE	Leaving twenty teenagers in a room with a DVD of *Braveheart*.
GEORGE	You did what?
	(BRIDIE *crosses to her desk and sorts papers and marker pens.* JIM *throws a pen across his desk.*)
JIM	Oh cheers, darlin'.
BRIDIE	(*to* BRIDIE) You need to talk to David. Something's not right. I thought he was your friend.
GEORGE	David is fine. There is nothing, absolutely nothing wrong with David.
BRIDIE	Then why is he lying on a rug on the back lawn making strange noises.
	(GEORGE *crosses to the window, followed by* JIM.)
GEORGE	Where?
JIM	What did I tell you, man? I've never seen him eat a pork pie neither.
	(JIM *moves away from the window.*)
BRIDIE	Come again?
GEORGE	(*shouting through the window*) LEAVE THAT NOW OLD MAN. THERE'S A MEETING. (*To* JIM.) He's rounding up the peacocks, you idiot.
	(GEORGE *moves away from the window,* JIM *takes his place and looks out.*)
JIM	Eh?

BRIDIE	Ruby's sealing off the dormitories and replacing all the whiteboards. There's new equipment for the gardeners and fresh paint on the walls. No wonder the Royals have a shaky grip on reality. They only ever see the display model.
GEORGE	You think Her Majesty should be treated to the septic tank and the mousetraps?
BRIDIE	No. Just the truth. The genuine version of the life that we live. The opinions we have. Where would be the harm in that?
GEORGE	It's all about presentation.
BRIDIE	Open your eyes.

(JIM *returns to his desk and sorts through his materials.*)

JIM	I'm all for it. She'll get a mouthful from me.
GEORGE	She will not.
JIM	Aye, well there's no need, is there. One glimpse of our monster-mooded Mickess will tell her all she needs to know.

(BRIDIE *yawns and stretches exaggeratedly.*)

JIM	Is baby tired?
BRIDIE	No baby's thirty-eight. Over-worked, stressed and totally disappointed in men. That's what baby is.
JIM	Baby needs a . . .
GEORGE	Stop it, the pair of you.
JIM	Watch your back, sister Celt. Mummy Moses is on the warpath. She suspects one of us of . . .

GEORGE	There's no need to worry Bridie. She's got her registers to sort out.

(GEORGE *drops registers on* BRIDIE*'s desk.*)

BRIDIE	No. Worry me. Please. I promise not to faint or become hysterical. Suspects one of us of what?
JIM	It's Ivor the Engine. He's spinning out of control. Chuffing up the wrong valley.

(*A silence.* BRIDIE *tries to decipher.*)

JIM	Dylan Thomas is helping himself from the optics. Tom Jones is robbing knickers from the line. It's time to get the male voice choir singing like canaries.
BRIDIE	What on God's earth does that pile of euphemistic sideways cobblers mean? No wonder we're in the mess we're in. No one knows what anybody is saying anymore.
GEORGE	Bridie, I . . .
JIM	Taffy was a Welshman. Taffy was a thief. Taffy came inside my house and stole a side of beef.
BRIDIE	SPEAK SODDING ENGLISH, WILL YA?
JIM	David's got his fingers in the till.
BRIDIE	No.
JIM	He's on the rob.
BRIDIE	David?
GEORGE	That is enough. Ridiculous. Given that Bridie's just about to have her flat repossessed it's more likely to be her.
BRIDIE	WHAT? Thank you, George. Thank you so much.

GEORGE	I thought it was common knowledge.
BRIDIE	It is now. Just what am I being accused of here?
GEORGE	Nothing. No one is. Drop it, Jim. Just . . .
JIM	Theft. The Earl's nick-nacks.
BRIDIE	There's a painting missing from my classroom. You think . . . you think David . . .
JIM	Look. Who's been behavin' oddly since St Patricks Day?
GEORGE	You spiked his drinks.
JIM	Who's just bought a new car?
GEORGE	A ten year old Mini Cooper with rusty hubcaps.
JIM	Who is endlessly making mystery phone calls?
BRIDIE	That's true. He does.
GEORGE	There's an explanation for . . .
JIM	Who pays cash for his refectory bill? Rest of us are on tick.
BRIDIE	He's never short. Very generous with the kiddies, too. Birthday cakes and prizes. You've noticed that, George.
GEORGE	Yes, but . . .
JIM	Who sneaks around after lights out? Eh – Bridie? Who tells us nothing about his weekends? Who plays it all close to his chest? Who watches and listens and gives nothing away. I'm telling you. It's him.

(DAVID *enters, mucky, still in his pyjamas and crosses to his desk.*)

DAVID Who'd have thought peacocks could be bribed with KFC? The bird kingdom has fallen prey to the lure of the Colonel's secret recipe. It'll be the invertebrates next. We won't be able to get out the door for slugs chomping on chicken nuggets. Has somebody died? Or is it me?

(*A silence.*)

GEORGE (*handing reports to* DAVID) Last weeks reports David. And I would really appreciate some appropriate clothes. Yes. Clothes would be good.

DAVID Okey-dokey. Should have a spare nano-second or two later.

GEORGE Let's just – all of us – let's just get on, shall we? Thank you.

(*A strange atmosphere prevails.* DAVID *gets on with his registers. All work silently – the work is boring but meticulous and demands concentration.* JIM *flicks an elastic band at* DAVID'S *head. One misses and hits* BRIDIE.)

BRIDIE Ouch. Nearly had my eye out.

JIM Watcha do at the weekend, David?

(BRIDIE *and* GEORGE *are interested in* DAVID'S *answer.*)

DAVID Sorry?

JIM Did you not understand the question?

DAVID You don't care what I did at the weekend.

JIM You never tell.

DAVID	You never ask.
JIM	I'm asking now.
DAVID	Is this a joke?
BRIDIE GEORGE JIM	No. No. No. Whatcha do?

(*A silence. All look at* DAVID.)

DAVID	Nothing. Nothing really.
JIM	(*clicking his fingers*) Yes.
BRIDIE	Proves nothing.

(GEORGE *wipes the whiteboard.* JIM *farts.*)

JIM	Better out than in, eh George?
GEORGE	What – it wasn't . . .

(BRIDIE *sorts through books.* JIM *leans back in his chair.*)

JIM	David.
GEORGE BRIDIE	Let's not . . . Leave him alone.
DAVID	Yes?
JIM	Have you got a boyfriend?
DAVID	Is that an offer?
JIM	And no family. No mates, as far as I can see.
BRIDIE	Shut up, will ya. Oh shit. (*She's made a mistake.*)
JIM	So who do you keep calling?

(*A silence. All look at* DAVID.)

DAVID No one.

JIM For someone who does nothing and sees no one you're a very busy man.

(GEORGE *crosses to the bell and rings it four times – one long, two short – one long – it's the break time bell sequence.*)

GEORGE Morning break. Wouldn't it be marvellous if we could work up to the end of the lessons? . . . As per contract.

(GEORGE *is ignored. Chairs can be heard scraping in the distance. He clears a space on the central table and begins to gather chairs around it. He doesn't see* JIM *draw a picture of a hot air balloon on the whiteboard with three stick figures in the basket. The hot air balloon approaches two mountains.*)

BRIDIE Any chance of nipping home at lunchtime? I'd like to change.

GEORGE No need. Anyway you look . . .

BRIDIE Yes?

GEORGE There's just no need. All will be revealed.

(BRIDIE *takes compact out of her bag and examines herself.*)

JIM David. Eyes up.

DAVID What?

GEORGE I just cleaned that.

JIM What is this?

(*A noise outside.* GEORGE *looks out of the window.*)

GEORGE   What the . . .

DAVID   It's a hot air balloon. Rapidly approaching some precipitous mountains.

GEORGE   Oh, not today. What the . . . Bridie. (*Shouting out of the window.*) HELLO – HELLO . . .

JIM   Indeed. Three immigrants are trying to make their way into the UK. They need to pass over the Grampians on their way to Hadrian's Wall and their final destination – Carlisle.

GEORGE   (*shouting off*) STOP THAT. STOP THAT IMMEDIATELY. DO YOU HEAR ME. STOP IT . . . Are they yours, Bridie? They're cartwheeling into the rhododendrons. Honestly.

JIM   We have immigrant A. A child prodigy violinist.

(BRIDIE *crosses to the window.* JIM *writes on the board.*)

JIM   Immigrant B. An aged doctor who has the cure for cancer and immigrant C. A black, pregnant woman.

BRIDIE   It's the French kids. (*Shouting through the window.*) MADEMOISELLE – PARDONEZ MOI, C'EST NE PAS PERMITTE . . . OUI . . . MERCI . . . Wow – look at that girl – she can flik-flack.

GEORGE   She can flik-flack all the way back to bloody Boulogne.

JIM   The balloon is too heavy. One of them has to jump. Which one?

GEORGE   Get her away from the bushes. She's got knees like razors. (*Shouting off.*) YOU – ALLEZ VITE A LA ... PAVEMENT AREA (*Running out of French.*) MOVE – JUST MOVE ...

BRIDIE   (*shouting through window*) OUI, JE CONNAIS – IL EST UN GRAND IDIOT ANGLAISE QUI PARLE BARVE ...

GEORGE   Don't encourage them, Bride.

DAVID   There's a dilemma.

GEORGE   They should be speaking English at all times.

BRIDIE   Take that as a thank you, shall I?

(BRIDIE *returns to her desk.*)

GEORGE   No – Yes – I don't know. Bridie ...

DAVID   One's a prodigy. One's got the cure for cancer. And one's black and pregnant.

JIM   Yes – who jumps?

GEORGE   What? What is this? Have you seen the time?

BRIDIE   Ethics the Scottish meathead way.

DAVID   If I had to choose I'd go for the child prodigy. Can't stand the violin and he's too young to know what he's missing.

JIM   A. You're sure?

DAVID   Yes.

JIM   OK. The kid jumps. They still can't clear the Grampians. Who's next?

DAVID   The Doctor. He's old. He's had the best of life.

JIM   But he's got the cure for cancer.

DAVID	Doubt that very much.
JIM	So B jumps. Leaving C. The black pregnant woman. Now why did you choose her David? Why did you save her?
DAVID	Two lives must equal more than one.
JIM	No other reason. Like an affinity.
DAVID	No, I've never been pregnant.
JIM	Fellow feeling. You know. Ancient stuff.
DAVID	Oh I see what you mean. No. Didn't cross my mind that she's . . .
BRIDIE	Give me that.

(BRIDIE *snatches the board rubber from* JIM *and wipes the board.*)

JIM	Hey.
BRIDIE	I reckon they were all black. And do you know what I'd say to them, Jim. All join hands and jump together while you'll still over the North Sea.

(BRIDIE *hands rubber back to* JIM.)

JIM	Palling up with him now, are you? Taking sides?
BRIDIE	No I am not. I am not on his side. Am I David?
DAVID	No she's not. She told me this morning.
GEORGE	What? What is going on here?
BRIDIE	But it's personal. Not general.
DAVID	No it's not. You generally don't like gay men.

BRIDIE	I didn't . . . I was . . .
GEORGE	Bridie?
BRIDIE	Look, there's a line. A line. There is a very definite line.
GEORGE	There most certainly is. There is a line.
BRIDIE	Yes. There's a line.
DAVID	Can somebody tell me where that line is please?
JIM	I'll tell you little man. It's a big fat line between debit and credit. Sinking and swimming. Living and dying and I for one cannot afford to lose my job. None of us can – right? So let's stop pissing about and call a spade a spade.

(RUBY *enters.*)

RUBY	Anyone calls anyone a spade around here and they're history. Where'dya learn your management skills George? Abu Ghraib?
GEORGE	I . . . it's just . . .

(RUBY *rings the bell four times.*)

RUBY	Gather round.
GEORGE	That bell is redundant.
RUBY	No it isn't, it shut you up. Sit down. We got ten minutes tops and I gotta run you through.

(*All move to their places around the table.*)

RUBY	Reports, please.

(GEORGE *hands papers to* RUBY.)

GEORGE	It's four for break time – one short – two long – one short – It's four long for lunch. You've

	just given the lunch bell five minutes into morning break.
RUBY	Don't have a kernipchen fit about your friggin' bell.
GEORGE	The Spanish will think it's time for a siesta. The Germans will look for a bus to board and the French will be ripping into baguettes and lolling on the grass. I've been ringing that bell for the past five years. It's about order. Leadership. You'll have anarchy on your hands but if that's what you want then fine. Fine.
JIM BRIDIE RUBY	No one listens to it anyway. I can't believe you're going off about the . . . Sit down, George, and shut up.

(GEORGE *slumps at the table.*)

RUBY	How in God's name did you ruckus-loving roughnecks ever conquer two thirds of the world?
DAVID	We were armed.
RUBY	A helicopter from the Queen's flight will be landing on the white 'H' out there at oh two hundred hours.
GEORGE	Two o'clock.
RUBY	Her Majesty will be meeted and greeted by . . .
GEORGE	MET. Met. Meet is an irregular verb.
RUBY	By yours truly. She will then be walked lickety-split across the lawn to . . .
GEORGE	I'm not sure Her Majesty should be lickety splat anywhere.
RUBY	To the podia out there.

GEORGE   Podium. Singular.

JIM   What podium?

RUBY   George is building it at lunchtime.

GEORGE   I'm what? I'm an MA.

BRIDIE   You're a TIT.

RUBY   You guys will be lined up in your glad rags ready to receive – that's e before i, George, in case you want to point it out – the Royal handshake.

BRIDIE   Glad rags? Hang on a minute. What glad rags?

GEORGE   We are supposed to teach correct usage. Your patois is confusing, Ruby.

RUBY   Hey. I'm from Queens. I speak Queens English. What's the problem?

BRIDIE ⎤   You are so petty.
GEORGE ⎥   The problem is the effect your . . .
JIM   ⎥   Let's just get on with it.
RUBY   ⎦   HEY HEY HEY. THAT'S ENOUGH.

RUBY   I quote . . . (*Reading.*) 'On presentation to the Queen the subject does not start the conversation.'

DAVID   Never thought of myself as a subject before.

JIM   Easy. You're as mysterious as maths and as tricky as Latin. With the deceit of drama thrown in.

BRIDIE   LEAVE HIM ALONE. Christ.

                (BRIDIE *crosses to her desk, picks up water and drinks.*)

JIM   Dehydrated?

BRIDIE	Get stuffed.

(BRIDIE *returns to the table.*)

RUBY	Her Majesty starts the conversation.
GEORGE	Will she ask anything challenging?
RUBY	Like what?
GEORGE	Something I can't answer.
JIM	Jesus, man, it couldn't be any easier. She comes with instructions.
BRIDIE	She's gonna talk about the weather.
DAVID	Why?
BRIDIE	She's English. It's the trick they all employ to avoid reality.
JIM	Actually she's German.
BRIDIE	Whatever, bonehead.
JIM	Thank Christ she's not Irish. She'd start the conversation with a punch. Beat herself up for ninety years and then roll over.
BRIDIE GEORGE DAVID RUBY	Shut your mouth you ignorant pig. Can we please approach this in a workmanlike … What's got in to everyone today? Hey. Hey. Hey.
RUBY	(*reading*) You will answer using in the first instance Her Majesty and thereafter Ma'am. Ma'am to rhyme with jam or bam …
JIM	(*looking at* DAVID) Or ham.
RUBY	Wham, bam, thank you ma'am. Clear?

BRIDIE	Yes, Ma'am.
DAVID	Ma'am.
JIM	Aye, Ma'am.
GEORGE	First Your Majesty then Ma'am. Yes. Clear.

BRIDIE   Do we have to curtsy?

JIM   I'm not curtsying to no one.

BRIDIE   Curtsying is for ladies.

JIM   Be bowing then, will you?

GEORGE   It's optional. I think. I read somewhere that . . .

DAVID   But we bow if we want to.

JIM   You can do a rain dance with a daffodil up your arse if the mood takes you.

BRIDIE   God almighty.

GEORGE   I think I'll nod. A fair compromise.

BRIDIE   That's right, George. You sit on that fence.

JIM   Give the lassie a drink. She's shaking.

RUBY   Once in 9C Jim will give his demonstration class to a group of students.

JIM   Tame ones. I don't want any froggy snail-eaters.

BRIDIE   Too far. Too bloody far.

GEORGE   French, Jim. French.

BRIDIE   That told him.

RUBY   Don't sweat the small stuff. The French ain't gonna play up in front of your Queen.

JIM	Didn't get much European history in your Hebrew school, did you?
RUBY	You don't get much Hebrew school if you got tits. Now shift your butt, loudmouth, and show us what you got.
JIM	What?
RUBY	You think I'm gonna let you loose on my financial future without a dry run? George. Takeover. I wanna observe.

(JIM *searches for his papers.*)

GEORGE	Oh. Right. Everyone up. Mock up of 9C please.

(*All arrange chairs in semi-circle around whiteboard and* GEORGE *picks up the print of the Queen.*)

GEORGE	So here's Her Majesty. Ruby and I escort her in. Eight students around the board. Bridie. David. You are pre-intermediates. Role-play please.

(DAVID *and* BRIDIE *sits as 'students'.*)

JIM	Don't crowd me. Fucking move back.
BRIDIE	I want my money back. Teacher is foul-mouthed fascist with small penis.
JIM	Suck it and see baby.
RUBY	Her Maj here has been pre-briefed. She knows Jim is teaching British culture with an emphasis on the class system.
GEORGE	What? He's teaching what?
RUBY	The bigwigs want to see we can hack the citizenship stuff. The big money is in citizenship.

GEORGE	But – We don't do – We do culture, custom and shopping. Yorkshire puddings and cream teas. Etiquette. Bowler hats and umbrellas. And. Yes. The weather.
RUBY	I want to see a lesson in democracy.
GEORGE	WHAT DO WE KNOW ABOUT SODDING DEMOCRACY?

(*A silence.*)

GEORGE	I mean . . . we do . . . but we can't teach it.
RUBY	Jim. Shoot.

(JIM *sets up his projector.*)

JIM	Good afternoon, students.
ALL	Good afternoon.
RUBY	George. George. Queen. Role-play.
GEORGE	What? Yes. Right. (*Queen impression – waving the print.*) Good afternoon, Jim. Please proceed.
JIM	Aye. Your Majesty.

(JIM *bows slightly.*)

BRIDIE	Bonnie Prince Charlie is spinning in his grave.
JIM	Shut up. Britain Today.

(*The words 'BRITAIN TODAY' appear.*)

GEORGE	Oh, God help us.

(*An image of a mansion appears.*)

JIM	Students. What kind of a house is this?

GEORGE	A stately home, teacher.
BRIDIE	A castle.
DAVID	A Premier League footballer's garden shed.
JIM	Like a stately home. A very big house. What's the word for these big houses? Come on. Christ.
RUBY	No cussin'.
GEORGE	A mansion.
JIM	Correct.

(*The word mansion appears under the image. Another image appears – a detached house.*)

JIM	What kind of a house is this?
BRIDIE	A mid eighties Barratt Executive containing an alcoholic housewife a bloated husband and enough synthetics to keep the petro-chemical industy afloat . . .
GEORGE	Bridie.
BRIDIE	A teenage son on crack cocaine and a neurotic Labrador.
GEORGE	Bridie.
BRIDIE	Suburban. It's a suburban house, teacher.
GEORGE	Modern.
JIM	There's a separate double garage and a garden.
BRIDIE	With a jacuzzi for alfresco wife-swapping parties.
JIM	It's on its own. It's free standing. IT'S ON its OWN.

DAVID   Detached.

JIM   Correct. Detached. A detached house.

(*The words 'detached house' appear beneath the image. Another image – a terraced house.*)

JIM   What kind of a house is this?

BRIDIE   We are going downmarket. It's a friggin' tip.

JIM   It's all I could find.

DAVID   A two-up, two-down.

BRIDIE   A turn of the century workman's cottage containing an exhausted supermarket worker with Chlamydia, an aggressive ex-con, twelve children, four of whom are pregnant, satellite TV and a freezer the size of Canada.

JIM   Tell her, George.

BRIDIE   A bouncy castle in the yard and six half-inched bicycles in the bathroom.

GEORGE   That is enough, Bridie.

JIM   What kind of a house is this? Is it on its own?

ALL   No.

JIM   Does it have a lovely garage and a lovely garden.

ALL   No.

DAVID   It's a terraced house. A terraced house.

JIM   A terraced house is correct.

(*The word terraced house appears under the image. The next image is that of the Queen.*)

GEORGE	Can we focus on the role-play please.
JIM	Now – who is this lovely lady?
RUBY	That is the magnificent and beautiful Queen Elizabeth the first, teacher.
JIM	No. No. Not Queen Elizabeth the First.
DAVID	Queen Elizabeth the First had red hair. They wouldn't let that happen now.
BRIDIE	Rubbish. Half the Royal Family are screaming gingers.
GEORGE	SOME RESPECT, PLEASE.
RUBY	Get a move on. You got three minutes.
JIM	Now where does she live? Here? Here? Or here?

(JIM *flicks through the images.*)

DAVID	Mansion, teacher.
JIM	Correct. She lives in several mansions. Can anyone name them?

(*The Queen's image appears next to that of the mansion.*)

GEORGE	Balmoral.
BRIDIE	Windsor castle. Sandringham. Buckingham Palace. They're palaces, not bloody mansions.
GEORGE	Let's not . . .
BRIDIE	It's the wrong word.
DAVID	Why does she have so many houses, teacher?

(*A silence.*)

JIM	What?
DAVID	I'm role-playing.
JIM	Answer him.
DAVID	It's exactly what they'll ask. Why?
JIM	Because . . . I cannae answer that. It's impossible.
GEORGE	Because so many people love her and she wants to live with them in many parts of the country.
BRIDIE	And the moon is made of Swiss cheese.
GEORGE	This Ruby is precisely why we don't . . . some things are best left unexamined. By foreigners. It's . . .
RUBY	The blue-blooded highness Dame is gonna be here in four hours. You wanna look like schmucks? Focus.

(JIM *calls up another image – a barrister in full fig.*)

JIM	How about this gentleman? What's his job?
BRIDIE	A lawyer.
DAVID	He's a barrister. Look at the wig.
JIM	And where does he live?
DAVID	In a large and beautifully decorated detached house just outside the North Circular.
JIM	Correct.
BRIDIE	Except at weekends when he shacks up with a lap dancer in Bethnal Green.

JIM	What is the point when all she's gonna do is . . .
GEORGE	Come on, Jim. Keep going. Just keep going.
RUBY	Carry on. Just carry on.
BRIDIE	Eh, David?

(The barrister's image is placed next to the detached house.)

JIM Detached is correct.

(The final image – a close-up of a black man in work-wear.)

JIM What is this man's job? Come on. What's this thing on his back with the rotten fruit and veg coming out of it.

GEORGE He's a bin-man. Great. We've got the gist. Ruby, can we . . .

RUBY No. Carry on.

BRIDIE Refuse Collector. The term now is Refuse Collector.

JIM Right and I'm a Language Facilitator and all that PC crap. He's a bin-man. Where does the bin man live?

GEORGE	In the terraced house.
DAVID	Terraced house.
BRIDIE	Terraced.

(The image appears next to the image of the terraced house.)

JIM Great. Nearly there now . . .

GEORGE Get a shake on, there's a good chap.

DAVID Why is he black?

(A silence.)

JIM	What? What did you say?
DAVID	Why is he black?
JIM	Is he black? I hadn't noticed.
BRIDIE	You liar.
GEORGE	Don't provoke him Bridie, for . . .
JIM	Aye aye, here we go. HERE WE GO. Saw it coming.
DAVID	Simple question.
JIM	This shite drives me nuts, you know it does.
DAVID	Why isn't the barrister black?
JIM	Jesus. Why isn't the Queen black?
DAVID	A black Head of State, wouldn't that be a fine thing?
JIM	Show me a black with the right credentials and I'll send the application form.
DAVID	Racist.
JIM	THAT IS OFFENSIVE. OFFENSIVE.
BRIDIE GEORGE JIM	Let it lie. Don't start on . . . Did you hear that? Did you all witness that? Did you hear what he just called me? A racist. Jesus Christ. MY BEST FRIEND IS SWEDISH.
BRIDIE	What?
DAVID	What's the problem? I'm only calling a spade a spade.

JIM	How dare you show me up in front of . . .
RUBY	Get on with it.
GEORGE	No. Don't ring the . . .

(RUBY *rings the bell several times.*)

RUBY   Thank you. The Regina is rapidly approaching.

GEORGE   I beg your pardon?

JIM   (*to* DAVID) One more word and your game is up. I'm warning you. Finally. We brainstorm a few character adjectives. Give me some adjectives to describe people like the Queen.

(*The Queen / Mansion image comes to the fore again. When* JIM *recognises a word which he has pre-programmed he flicks his switch and it comes up on the screen.*)

RUBY	Rich.
GEORGE	Powerful. Proud. Superior.

BRIDIE   Your Knighthood's in the bag.

GEORGE	Privileged. Regal. Gracious.
BRIDIE	Gorgeous. Delightful. Tremendous.

BRIDIE   Simply sublime.

JIM   OK. Same again for our Barrister.

(*The Barrister / detached house image comes to the fore.*)

GEORGE	Educated. Professional. Well-off.
BRIDIE	Comfortable. Charming. Well-fed.

GEORGE   Ambitious. Accomplished.

JIM   Yes.

GEORGE   Dedicated.

JIM Good. And how about our bin-man?

(*The bin-man image comes to the fore.*)

BRIDIE Poor. Unhealthy. Hard-working.

GEORGE Sad. He looks sad. Terrible photo, Jim. There are better ones in the . . .

JIM Sad is a weak adjective like nice. Let's have something stronger.

BRIDIE Miserable.

JIM Good.

(*The adjectives appear next to the image.*)

DAVID Silenced. Angry and dangerous.

(*A silence.* JIM *slams his fist down on the desk.*)

JIM And best ignored . . . There's a word for each of these groups in Britain. What is that word in each case?

(*Each row of places / people / adjectives is highlighted. The appropriate 'class' flashes up in each case.*)

GEORGE Upper class.

JIM Correct. And this one?

GEORGE Middle class.

JIM Correct. And lastly . . .

GEORGE Working class. Jolly good. The Queen is highly impressed now can we . . .

JIM Don't keep interrupting me, you.

| GEORGE | I think we should . . .
| BRIDIE | Leave him be.
| RUBY | Carry on.

JIM Finally the writing homework. IF – to revise the second conditional – YOU WERE BRITISH (*Sentence appearing.*) WHICH CLASS WOULD YOU CHOOSE TO BELONG TO AND WHY?

(*A silence.*)

DAVID I'd choose land-owning gentry. I'd choose the opening of doors and the receipt of respect. I'd choose white skin a fat bank balance and a heterosexual interest in Christina Aguilera. I'd choose any sodding class but yours, teacher.

JIM I warned you. Don't say I didn't warn you . . .

(*The distant sound of a Chinook helicopter.*)

| GEORGE | What?
| BRIDIE | Jesus . . .
| RUBY | That is enough.

(RUBY *flicks on the side lights and turns off the projector.*)

JIM Here is your thief, Ruby. Here's your marked man. Here's the nigger in the fucking woodpile.

| GEORGE | You can't say . . . what the hell was that?
| BRIDIE | That is outrageous . . . oh my God.
| RUBY | I said that is enough.

(*The Chinook swoops very low over the house. Lights flicker. A deafening noise.* BRIDIE, GEORGE, RUBY *and* JIM *head to the window. A sudden load deceleration and crunching outside.*)

GEORGE	Oh my God. Oh my God. It's landed on the pergola.
BRIDIE	What the . . . It's the friggin' army.
JIM	What the . . .

(JIM *moves to the window.*)

GEORGE The pergola. It's landed on the pergola.

RUBY No sweat. It's just the soldiers.

BRIDIE Soldiers? What friggin' soldiers?

GEORGE They're American. What the hell are American soldiers doing on our croquet lawn?

RUBY Helping you guys out. Aintcha heard? We're allies.

BRIDIE We're being invaded.

GEORGE They've destroyed a piece of Art Deco architecture.

RUBY They're here to protect the sovereign. It's the price of security, George.

GEORGE Vandalism? Mindlessness? Chaos? There's a white 'H' out there the size of Venuezala. What are they doing? What in God's name do they think they are doing . . .

(GEORGE *exits blowing his whistle.*)

RUBY It's special measures. For the visit. Just get out there.

BRIDIE Don't mess with them, George. GEORGE.

(BRIDIE *exits.*)

RUBY Don't panic. We need to clear up the mess is all. You too, Columbo – I'll deal with you later.

JIM	I'm telling you he is . . .
RUBY	Where's ya proof? MOVE IT.

(RUBY *pushes* JIM *out of the door. The sounds of consternation outside.*)

RUBY An Englishman, an Irishwoman, a Scotsman and a Welshman run an English school. What is this? Some kind of a joke.

(BRIDIE, GEORGE *and* JIM *appear through the window.*)

ALL RUBY!

(RUBY *exits.*)

DAVID I'm not laughing any more.

(*Blackout.*)

ACT TWO

Scene One

The same – 1:45 PM. The sound of a helicopter passing overhead.

The gun display case is empty, glass completely gone.

Bridie, *tearful, in Irish National Costume attempts a few bars on the penny whistle. She gives up, finds a bottle in her drawer and pours a large glass. She drinks. She tries the penny whistle again.*

Bridie	Jesus, Mary, Michael and Joseph. I can't do it. I can't.
	(*She gives up, tearful.* Jim *appears in the doorway in full kilt, sporran and dress shirt, a jemmy tucked into his waistband.*)
Jim	If a man says something in the woods and there's no woman around is he still wrong?
Bridie	If I throw you a stick will you go away?
	(Bridie *turns round to see* Jim.)
Bridie	Oh my God. It's a giant baby in a travel rug. I didn't know you could play the . . .
Jim	I cannae. Ruby wants the full effect, you know. The image.
Bridie	The Irish invented bagpipes and gave them to the Scottish as a joke. Only the Scottish never got it.
Jim	Don't you mock. Men have died to wear the kilt.
Bridie	Why didn't they just pick up a micro-mini at Dorothy Perkins.
Jim	Are you dancing a jig for us?

BRIDIE	I'm teaching the kids. Badly. Folk songs and the like. Ruby thinks being Irish is enough. I move like John McCririck sing like Lee Marvin and I'm tone deaf.
JIM	Have you heard about the Irish boomerang? Doesn't come back. Just sings songs about how much it wants to.
BRIDIE	What's black and blue and floats in the river? A Scotsman telling Irish jokes. Stop, it Jim. I've had it up to here. I'm dressed up like an invitation to a ceilidh my hearts aching and David's disappeared.
	(BRIDIE *takes a drink.*)
JIM	What a treat for the Queen. A leprechaun on the lash.
BRIDIE	Beats a caveman in a skirt. Do you know how much trouble you've caused?
JIM	Me? I've nae light fingers.
BRIDIE	Just a light brain. And a disgusting foul mouth.
JIM	It slipped out, that's all. Heat of the moment. It's a turn of phrase. Christ, all I heard when I was a bairn. You think I'm ripe, you should have met my old man. Would have made Alf Garnet blush. Yours, too, no doubt. Old habits die hard. Old language lingers. It's just words. Words can't harm us. Words don't chain us up. Words don't kill.
BRIDIE	A closed mouth gathers no foot.
JIM	That what you want? A world full of muted assassins? Smiling peace. Thinking treason.
	(JIM *picks at the locks on* DAVID'S *drawers with his dirk.*)

BRIDIE   What are you doing? That's David's desk.

JIM   Wouldn't you know it. It's an Aladdin's cave. Paper. (*He throws items onto the desktop.*) Envelopes. Six marker pens fresh in their packet and a bumper pack of paper clips.

                (BRIDIE *opens her drawer.*)

BRIDIE   Two reams of paper. Three board rubbers. Ten first-class stamps and five sachets of sugar. Be joining David on the scaffold, will I?

JIM   There's more. There must be more. I cannae open this cupboard.

                (JIM *tries to force* DAVID's *desk.*)

RUBY   (*on PA*) Attention. Attention students. Her Majesty the Queen arrives in ten minutes. Take your positions. I repeat. Take your positions.

BRIDIE   Ten minutes. What are you – you need your head examined.

JIM   No. I need a jemmy.

BRIDIE   Shush. What's that?

                (JIM *and* BRIDIE *listen to the sound of approaching bells.* GEORGE *appears in the doorway, wearing a Morris Dancer's costume complete with blown-up condom to replicate a pig's bladder.*)

BRIDIE ⎤   What the . . .
JIM   ⎦   Christ, George.

                (GEORGE *takes a couple of steps into the room.*)

GEORGE   Ah. I was hoping to surprise you.

BRIDIE   Fat chance.

JIM	Why have you got a blown up rubber jonnie hanging off your belt?
BRIDIE	What?
GEORGE	Yes. Effective, don't you . . . Cook couldn't muster a pig's bladder.
BRIDIE	Thank God.
GEORGE	Tricky. We English . . . what's the national costume? It was either a morris dancer, a beefeater or a football-shirted psychopath with tattoos and a can of Special Brew. I thought this was the best option.
BRIDIE	Look what Ruby's done to us, George. We're Disney characters. Where's our friggin' dignity?
GEORGE	Needs must . . . it's a PR exercise, Bridie. Marketing. For the brochures. It'll play brilliantly abroad. England, Ireland, Wales and Scotland meet the Queen.
BRIDIE	Only Wales has fallen off the map.
RUBY	(*on PA*) WHERE ARE YOU? FIVE MINUTES AND COUNTING. I SAID STAND BY SO FRIGGIN' WELL STAND BY.
JIM	Not before I've sorted this out.
	(JIM *exits.*)
GEORGE	Let's give them five for assembly. That should do it.
	(GEORGE *gives five rings on the bell.*)
GEORGE	Come on, Bridie. The choir's gathered. Put on a good show, shall we? Bit silly, but – I've always wanted to meet the . . .

(BRIDIE *slumps at her desk.*)

GEORGE
: What on earth is the matter? (*Anxiously checking his watch.*)

BRIDIE
: I can't play the penny whistle.

GEORGE
: Oh. I see. Bridie we really need to . . .

BRIDIE
: I can't sing. And I can't dance like Michael Flatley.

GEORGE
: There's no time for . . .

BRIDIE
: I'm useless. And all I need. All I want. Is to be loved.

GEORGE
: Right. Well, I . . . I . . . I can't love you until 3:45. Will it keep?

(BRIDIE *collapses in tears.* GEORGE *approaches, jangling and pulls up a chair next to* BRIDIE.)

GEORGE
: Now . . . now buck up. Yes? Stiff upper lip. Deep breath. Chin up and into the handshaking fray.

(BRIDIE *tries.*)

BRIDIE
: It's not working.

(GEORGE *spots the glass on* BRIDIE'S *desk.*)

GEORGE
: Have you been drinking?

BRIDIE
: What do you care?

GEORGE
: I care. I do care, Bridie. I really do.

BRIDIE
: It's all my fault.

GEORGE
: No. We can't all be musically gifted.

BRIDIE	I was frustrated. He was an easy target. And now everybody hates him. What have I done?
GEORGE	There. There. It took me three years to master Chopsticks.
BRIDIE	It's because . . . it's because I . . . I love you.
GEORGE	And that was just the left hand.
BRIDIE	Tell me. Tell me you have . . . feelings for me, George.

(*A silence.*)

GEORGE	I . . .
BRIDIE	Yes?

(GEORGE *takes* BRIDIE'S *hand.*)

GEORGE	I think you're a very . . . very . . .
BRIDIE	Yes?
JIM	Got one.

(JIM *enters with a jemmy and approaches* DAVID'S *cupboard.*)

GEORGE	Good teacher.

(GEORGE *slaps* BRIDIE *heartily on the back and leaps up.*)

GEORGE	And we all need to be on the ball. Yes. The Queen is coming. How . . . exciting. And I think we all look . . . yes. Don't we. What are you doing? Jim. Jim.
JIM	What you should be doing. Getting to the bottom of things. Taking action. Checking Davey Jones' locker.

                    (JIM *works on* DAVID'S *cupboard with the jemmy.*)

GEORGE   It would be more helpful to find him.

BRIDIE   We've looked. Looked and looked and looked.

RUBY   (*on PA*) TEACHERS. TEACHERS WHERE ARE YA? I WANT YOU OUT FRONT NOW.

GEORGE   Leave it, Jim. Chop-chop everybody. This is it. This is it.

                    (JIM *opens* DAVID'S *cupboard with a loud crack.*)

BRIDIE   God almighty.
JIM   YES.
GEORGE   Please, Jim. I'm begging you. Let's just . . .

                    (JIM *finds a small canvas and unrolls it.*)

JIM   Well, well, well.

                    (RUBY *enters dressed to the hilt in a huge hat and gloves.*)

RUBY   What in the hell is going on? You got a tableau to slot into.

GEORGE   It's an oil painting.

RUBY   Why thank you, George. What's a Jewish woman's favourite position? On the designer floor at Harrods.

JIM   Here's your proof, Ruby. Inside David's desk. Now we can get back to some sort of normality and stability. Here is your proof.

                    (*The sound of a helicopter approaching.*)

GEORGE   What? I don't understand. He . . .

RUBY	Hand it over. And get outside, the lot of you. Now. Move it.
BRIDIE	(*to* JIM) I hope you're happy now.
JIM	(*handing the canvas over to* RUBY) Wham, Bam thank you Ma'am.

(JIM *exits.*)

RUBY	AND SMILE – A TRIUMPHANT REGINA IS LANDING ON THE LAWN.
GEORGE	WILL YOU STOP SAYING THAT. We don't talk about reginas.
RUBY	So it's David.
GEORGE	Her Majesty is not a . . . not in the vernacular. It's official. For coins . . .
RUBY	Is that right? Our thief. It's David.

(*A silence.*)

GEORGE	What? Yes. It's David.
RUBY	We have a name. Woop-di-do. Just get it together get out there and make nice with Queen. NOW.

(RUBY *exits.* GEORGE *stands stunned at himself. He crosses to the mirror. He looks at himself, smoothing his hair.*)

BRIDIE, JIM *and* RUBY'S *legs appear on the podia.*)

GEORGE	Come on, George. You're a decent chap. Whatever the choices you've made. Whatever the mistakes. Whatever the failings. You've done it for the greater good. You've done it for the College. For the kid. And for England.

(GEORGE moves away from the mirror and crunches on some glass. He looks down. He looks up at the gun display case and gasps as he notices it's empty. He puts his hand through the non-existent glass just as DAVID appears from his hiding place in the corner of the room where he's stood unnoticed all this time. The sound of a helicopter landing.)

DAVID And you really believe that, don't you?

GEORGE David – what the . . . you . . . the . . . it's . . . missing.

DAVID Fancy that. Our thief has been at it again.

GEORGE Yes – No. David . . . I . . . look at the state of you . . .

RUBY *(off)* GEORGE, GET OUT HERE NOW.

(The sound of the band attempting a Royal herald.)

GEORGE I'm going to lock you in. For your own good.

DAVID A citizen's arrest is it?

GEORGE No . . . no . . . I'll . . . I'll do something. I swear. I believe in fair play, you know. Fair play. Just keep quiet, there's a good chap. I'll keep you posted.

(GEORGE closes the door and locks it from the outside.)

DAVID Don't think so, George. Today Wales is gonna make a very big noise indeed.

RUBY *(off)* STRIKE UP THE BAND.

(DAVID sits with a view through the window and slowly unwraps his parcel on his desk.

>   RUBY, BRIDIE *and* JIM'S *legs can be seen
>   nervously waiting in line to meet the Queen.*
>   GEORGE'S *legs join them, tripping on the way.
>   The band strikes up 'God Save The Queen' and
>   a group of foreign learners can be heard
>   singing very badly.*)

GEORGE (*bending down to speak to* DAVID) Any minute now. Any minute now. And OH MY GOD. She's coming. She's coming this way. No she's stopped. She's waving. She's waving, David.

DAVID Waving. Right.

GEORGE She's . . . now she's walking. She's walking, David.

DAVID Walking *and* waving? Give the woman a pay rise.

GEORGE She looks stunning. Absolutely . . . gracious. Very gracious. Floating almost. In fuchsia. Radiant. Smiling. Enormous handbag. Surprisingly large boobs. She looks . . . Magnificent. David – David can you hear me?

DAVID Loud and clear.

> (DAVID *raises his gun so that* GEORGE *can see
> him putting bullets into the chamber of the
> gun.*)

GEORGE What the . . . YOU'VE GOT THE . . .

DAVID Gun, yes.

GEORGE AND YOU'VE GOT . . .

DAVID Bullets too, yes. Internet. A modern miracle.

GEORGE Oh my God. Oh my God. Do nothing. I'm on my way. Two tics and I'll . . . DON'T MOVE A MUSCLE.

(The band plays 'The Star Spangled Banner'. The Queen's legs and corgis' feet can be seen approaching the receiving line. DAVID pours himself a glass of whisky from BRIDIE'S desk.)

GEORGE JUST KEEP CALM. KEEP ... OW.

(RUBY, unseen, yanks GEORGE up. The Queen's legs stop at RUBY, who curtsies.)

DAVID I am calm, George. Calmer than I have been for years. Today is the day. The day I've been waiting for. The day I make my mark.

(GEORGE'S head re-appears. DAVID sits in his chair, gun across his chest.)

GEORGE Put it down, David. Plea ...

(RUBY once again yanks GEORGE up.)

DAVID Can't do that, George. Sorry.

(The band strikes up 'Danny Boy' as the Royal party approaches JIM.)

GEORGE *(bending down)* We can work this out.

DAVID Lennon and McCartney were wrong. We can't.

GEORGE What?

DAVID Work anything out. Not any more.

(The band segues into a vibrant version of 'The Irish Washer Woman' and the Queen moves to BRIDIE, who takes a deep unsteady curtsy, wobbles and drops to a knee, and is rapidly pulled up into the standing position. The band bursts into a loud and tuneless version of 'English Country Garden' as the party moves towards GEORGE. A corgi raises it's leg against GEORGE'S trouser. There is a moment's consternation and the music drones

into nothingness as dogs bark and there is general kerfuffle. DAVID *stands and finds various doors books and items of furniture to punctuate and keep rhythm with his singing.*)

DAVID (*singing loudly*) 'Men of Harlech march to glory, Victory is hoverin' o'er ye, Bright eyed freedom stands afore ye . . .

(BRIDIE *bends down and sees* DAVID. *She pulls at* JIM *who similarly bends down, followed by* RUBY *and* GEORGE.)

BRIDIE ⎤ David? What's that – he's got a . . .
JIM ⎥ Bloody hell. He's lost it . . .
RUBY ⎦ What the – Get in there, George.

(*All heads go back up apart from* GEORGE'S.)

GEORGE MUSIC. MUSIC NOW.

(GEORGE *stands and his legs are seen moving along the line towards the house.* JIM *and* RUBY'S *feet move off the podia to be replaced by foreign student Irish Dancers' feet.*)

DAVID 'Wales ne'er will yield'.

GEORGE (*off*) MUSIC NOW, FOR GODS SAKE.

(*The band strikes up – very loud Irish folk dancing music – and the badly taught feet begin to dance. The key rattles in the lock.* DAVID *points the gun at the door as* GEORGE *bursts in, locking it behind him and trousering the key.*)

GEORGE DON'T SHOOT. DON'T SHOOT ME. I . . . I am the father of a clinically obese eight year old. My life has a purpose.

DAVID Providing a market for the fast food industry.

GEORGE	Put it down, David. Let's talk. Please put it down.
DAVID	No. That would be daft. Even for a Welshman.
GEORGE	Right.
DAVID	Even for a black man.
GEORGE	Point taken.
DAVID	Even for a great big limp-wristed arse-bandit.
GEORGE	I've never thought of you . . . as anything other than an honest hard-working honourable chap. Bright. Sensitive. Team player.
DAVID	Thinking it isn't enough, George. No one can hear it, see. Gotta be heard. It's all gotta be heard.
GEORGE ⎤ DAVID ⎦	Yes. Yes. Sit down.

(GEORGE *sits, hands above his head.*)

GEORGE	Works, does it? The . . . gun. Tested it, have you? Been a few years since it started the first world war.
DAVID	Who fired it?
GEORGE	What?
DAVID	Am I standing on the shoulder of a giant? TELL ME.
GEORGE	Alright. Alright, don't . . . Gavrilo Princip. Son of a postman.
DAVID	My Dad, too. Fancy that.

GEORGE	A Serbian Nationalist who wanted independence from Austria.
DAVID	Really?
GEORGE	They caught him. He got twenty years. Only served four . . . He . . . died . . . been ill for a long time. TB.
DAVID	A man at the end of his rope. Happy to die for his cause. To go down and take everybody with him.
GEORGE	The doctor . . . You . . . Oh God . . . I had no time. David, I . . .
DAVID	Has a funny way of repeating itself. History. Doesn't it?
GEORGE	Enough. Enough of this nonsense.

(GEORGE *approaches* DAVID.)

DAVID	Sit down. What are you doing?
GEORGE	There are dozens of security men out there. Not to mention American soldiers.
DAVID	You're safer in here then.
GEORGE	You can't succeed. Give me the gun.
DAVID	Don't underestimate the determination of the disenfranchised.
GEORGE	I refuse to discuss disenfranchisement with the Queen on the premises.
DAVID	When would be a good time?
GEORGE	Give it to me, there's a good chap.
DAVID	Can I make an appointment?

GEORGE   There is no need for you to do yourself any harm.

DAVID   Now *there* is an assumption, George.

(*A silence.*)

GEORGE   What? What do you . . .

(*The music stops.* BRIDIE *leans down.*)

BRIDIE   What in the hell is going on? Have you lost your mind, David?

GEORGE   Carry on as normal, Bridie. Carry on. Carry on.

(BRIDIE *stands up again.*)

BRIDIE   Normal? I've forgotten what normal is. (*Off.*) YOUR MAJESTY. LADIES AND GENTLEMEN. THE PENNY WHISTLE.

(BRIDIE *plays the penny whistle.*)

DAVID   I gave you a chance this morning, George. I tried to talk to you. But you don't want us Welsh talking. Only listening.

GEORGE   That's not . . . what is this? Revolution.

DAVID   Right now, it's civil war.

GEORGE   Ranting and raving like a bolshie undergrad will get you nowhere.

DAVID   Oh, I know I should have fallen asleep years ago. When I realised the doors would never open for me. That I wasn't going to be one of those bloated academics with lazy letters after my name, lolling around in an armchair spouting Shakespeare and taking my acolytes up the arse.

GEORGE	Some academics are heterosexual and there's no need to be vulgar.
DAVID	Oh for . . .
GEORGE	What have I ever done apart from be your friend?
DAVID	NOTHING. AND NOTHING ISN'T ENOUGH.

(DAVID *kicks a chair towards* GEORGE.)

GEORGE	Steady. Steady. Calm down, David. You're obviously not . . . at your best, old man. Bad news. You're a bit depressed.
DAVID	Giving something a name doesn't make it go away. Look at Al Qaeda.
GEORGE	I'm not bandying semantics with a mad man.
DAVID	I'm not mad. I'm fucking furious.

(RUBY'S *face appears in the window.*)

RUBY	George. Lock him in and get your butt out here. I want the cricket demonstration. NOW.

(RUBY *stands and her legs and the Queen's legs indicate the dishing out of certificates to a selection of students' legs.* GEORGE *approaches* DAVID.)

GEORGE	What's your plan?
DAVID	I didn't write one up for this particular lesson.
GEORGE	We can sort this out. Rationally. Sit down. Thrash it out, come to mutually acceptable terms and shake on it.
DAVID	It's you who needs the doctor.

GEORGE You are going to come to your senses. You hear me? Think about what you stand to lose.

DAVID Heartache . . . thanklessness – and betrayal. (*Lifting the rolled up canvas*).

(*A silence.*)

GEORGE I . . . I'm sorry.

(GEORGE *exits and locks the door behind him.* DAVID *puts the gun down and takes a drink from the whisky bottle. Outside,* RUBY *announces the cricket match. Two chairs are placed side by side on the podia and* RUBY *sits next to the Queen and her corgi to watch play. The sound of a ball being hit by a cricket bat.*)

DAVID (*shouting off*) KEEP A STRAIGHT BAT, EH GEORGE?

(*The key turns in the lock.* BRIDIE *enters.* DAVID *picks up the gun.*)

BRIDIE It's me. Bridie.

DAVID What is this – a fancy dress relay?

BRIDIE The hot-headed drivel-talking idiot. Don't shoot me. Please don't shoot. A fellow Celt counts as an own goal.

DAVID I'm your fellow nothing, pet.

BRIDIE David, I swear. If I still went to church. If I still believed in God and if I hadn't had a drink I would go confess right now and be on my knees for the next month about what I said this morning. I can't live with the guilt.

DAVID Thought it was the guilt that kept your lot going. Close the door. And lock it.

(BRIDIE *closes and locks the door.*)

BRIDIE	I do quite like home make-over programmes and I've been to see *Mamma Mia*. Just stop it now, please. It's all got out of hand.
DAVID	It does, Bridie. Don't you see? Take what you said this morning. Multiply it by a million. Add a portion of physical abuse and a side order of bullying and you're tuckin' in the plateful I've had.
BRIDIE	Get out of it then. There's no need for this . . . insanity. I can't believe I've just done a dancing fairy act for the British Monarchy. I'm leaving. I'm going.
DAVID	What? You can't.
BRIDIE	I fancy a school in central London. Concrete. No culture and no bloody history. And no George.
DAVID	You'll kill him. Sooner than I might.
BRIDIE	What?
DAVID	He loves you, Bridie.
	(*A thwack of a cricket ball being hit. A smattering of applause.*)
DAVID	You've hit him for six. He watches you, you know. Watches you move. Watches you breathe. He stands behind the frosted glass outside room seven. Traces the silhouette of your body in the dust on the frame. He writes e-mails from you to him and reads them back to himself at lunchtime. He talks to you when you're not here and cocks his head to hear your answer. He sits in your chair and closes his eyes and sometimes he smells that old scarf you leave hanging on the back of the door. He winces when you bump into something and his cheeks go pink when you laugh. He lives to see

	you every morning. He has a deep need for you. He loves each and every atom of you. His atoms are blown apart and burning with desire for you. He's taken. He's yours . . . You win.
BRIDIE	David . . .
DAVID	I knew there was no hope, but . . .
BRIDIE	I had no idea.
DAVID	No. None us have any idea, do we? About anything. Because we don't speak to each other. We exchange insults. Punch each other with painful jokes. Use this beautiful, beautiful, expressive, expansive, enviable language as a disguise. A deceit. Our Queen's English is an instrument of torture, teasing and suggesting and misleading and provoking. Why not just say it? I LOVE GEORGE. YOU LOVE GEORGE AND HE . . . LOVES . . . YOU . . .
	(JIM *hammers heavily at the door.*)
JIM	(*off*) Open up. Open up I say.
DAVID	AND I HATE HIM.
	(DAVID *picks up his gun.*)
BRIDIE	No. No, David, please. GO AWAY JIM. Leave the gun. Please. Let's talk.
	(DAVID *points the gun at* BRIDIE.)
BRIDIE	No. No, please.
JIM	(*hammering on the door*) BRIDIE – you alright in there? Open up.
	(*A sudden yell of 'Owzat' and applause outside distracts* DAVID. BRIDIE *rushes to the door and opens it.* JIM *rushes in and grabs* BRIDIE.)

JIM	Get out. Get out now. This is no place for a woman.
BRIDIE	For once, I agree with you.

(BRIDIE *exits.* JIM *closes the door and locks it. He and* DAVID *play silent cat-and-mouse around the room. Finally* DAVID *mounts the cupboards and manages to get the gun to* JIM's *head.*)

JIM	Didn't know you were such a Gurkha. Should join me and the lads. Channel some of that aggression.
DAVID	I am channelling it, Jim. Right down the barrel of a gun. Sit down.

(DAVID *manoeuvres* JIM *into a chair and he sits. He reaches for his sporran.*)

DAVID	Don't move.
JIM	I wanna smoke.

(DAVID *takes the sporran, finds cigarettes and lighter and hands them to* JIM. DAVID *holds the gun close to* JIM's *head.*)

JIM	Easy. Easy. Her Majesty the Queen would like to know where Wales is.
DAVID	So what's new?
JIM	An Englishman, an Irishwoman, a Scotsman and a Welshman . . .
DAVID	You have got to be joking.
JIM	They meet at an interview for a job. None of them gets it. They adjourn to the pub. The Irish woman's been sacked from every job she's ever had . . .

DAVID	Is this a shaggy-dog story?
JIM	The Welshman's a moody so-and-so and the Scotsman's a reject from the army without a penny to his name. The Englishman wants to be flash so he buys them all a drink. An idea is born. The Englishman has a contact. A batty old aristocrat with a pile he can't afford to maintain. The four of them take on the lease and the United School of English is born.
DAVID	Should stick to one-liners, Jim. You're losing me.
JIM	Each one has the National traits you'd expect. George is an ineffectual overly polite twat. Bridie is a wild eyed neurotic drunk. I'm a straight talking tough guy . . .
DAVID	Uh huh.
JIM	And you're well . . . you're . . .
DAVID	All begins to fall down a bit over here doesn't it?
JIM	No. You're still a grumpy animal-boffin' inbred, only you've been modernised somewhat.
DAVID	I see.
JIM	On account of the deep tan and being a Muslim.
DAVID	Closest I've ever been to Mecca is the bingo hall.
JIM	We all, all of us, bite the bullet for sake of expediency. Profit and security. I mean Christ, none of us actually like each other do we? Well do we?
DAVID	And the punchline?

JIM	We like our own kind. It's a universal truth. We hate everybody else.
DAVID	That's it?
JIM	And now Ruby's involved. Sticking her nose in. Stirring it up. I ask you . . . What does a Jewish American woman know about centuries of enmity and hatred?

(DAVID *grabs a chair and sits very close to* JIM.)

JIM	What you doing?
DAVID	Thinking about the best way to hurt you. To pay you back for every sick joke. Every ignorant remark. Every jibe and every quip.
JIM	Give over. You give as good as you get.
DAVID	I've fantasised about blowing your head off. Sticking a gun in your ear. (*He does so.*) Pulling the trigger back and . . .
JIM	Go on. Go on then. Do your worst, you grubby little shit. Be a man. Be a man for once. Do it. What are you waiting for? Get me. COME ON GET ME. Rip me apart. BLOW ME AWAY.

(*Quickly* DAVID *drops the gun, grabs his head and kisses him on the mouth.* JIM *goes rigid for moment, then relaxes.* DAVID *stops kissing* JIM *and moves away. Another round of applause from the cricket spectators outside.* JIM *gets smaller.* RUBY'S *feet move away from beside the Queen.*)

DAVID	I love George. George loves Bridie. Bridie loves him back. And you love me. Don't you. Love me so much you want me out of the way. Tough, isn't it, Jim? Being honest.
JIM	How do you get . . . How do you get four poufs on a bar stool? Turn it over and press down hard.

(DAVID *laughs. Louder and louder until* JIM *can't stand it and heads for the door.* RUBY *meets him in the doorway.*)

RUBY Wassamatta Arnie? You didn't get the bad guy?

JIM Ruby, I . . .

RUBY George and Her Maj are waiting for your teaching demo in 7C. Go give her the lowdown on the houses and the classes and the whole citizenship fandango.

JIM I can't . . . I cannae teach, I . . . I'm all churned up . . . I cannae . . .

RUBY Skiddaddle. David and I are gonna take a stroll down Amicable Avenue. Now shoot. Not you. Him. I won't ask twice.

JIM This is . . . this is a joke.

RUBY No. This a joke. What do you call a Scotsman with . . . hey . . .

(JIM *runs off.*)

RUBY With half a brain. Gifted. (*Picking up* JIM'S *sporran.*) YOU FORGOT THE FURRY CLUTCHBAG.

(RUBY *locks the door, crosses to a chair and takes off her shoes.*)

RUBY I swear, no more high heels. Could be a meet with the almighty himself but this dame'll be in mules and corn plasters. She's a sweet little lady. Your Lizzie. She and I share a mutual liking for chopped liver and Neil Diamond.

DAVID Is that right?

RUBY	Yeah. She told me. She and the Greek guy jump on their geegees and sing 'Forever in Blue Jeans' together. Ain't that sweet?
DAVID	Going on the payroll, is she?
RUBY	Don't be ridiculous she's state-funded. You need a figurehead kid. You gotta have one. Hell, you can have ours if you prefer. He comes with Boss eyes and the intellect of a Hershey bar but he can handle the smiling and the waving just the same. So. How long you got?
DAVID	What?
RUBY	I know you're sick. I know you went to the Doc. I know it was bad news this morning.
DAVID	Very perceptive of you.
RUBY	No. I got the joint wired.
DAVID	What? You can hear what we . . .
RUBY	Look, I just did back flips of politeness and all the English baloney – let's cut the crap.
DAVID	A year. Maybe two.
RUBY	Oi ya, oi. That's long enough to live it up in San Fran, write a book in Greenwich village and go to Sante Fe for a salt beef sandwich.
DAVID	I don't want to.
RUBY	But you could, kid. That's the point. You are in a great position.
DAVID	What?
RUBY	Most of us don't know when the final drum roll's gonna come. Could be sittin' on our butts watching daytime. We could choke on a jello sandwich. Could get blown outta da sky in an

	aeroplane. Unprepared. Instant. Gone. But you – you got two years. It's like a package trip with no return date. Put your plaid pants on and party.
DAVID	No. I want to change things.
RUBY	So you're gonna use the metal banana on a cuddly old grandma who knows all the words to 'Sweet Caroline?'
	(*A silence.* DAVID *lowers the gun and puts it on the desk in front of him. He sits, deflated.*)
RUBY	Attaboy.
DAVID	My whole life has been the butt of a joke.
RUBY	You don't say.
DAVID	Black this. Gay that. Welsh is the icing on the cake. Got me down as Muslim now. A crook too. The Earl gave me this painting. As a gift.
RUBY	Thought as much. What is George's game?
DAVID	The Earl liked me.
RUBY	He ain't the only one, kiddo.
DAVID	Don't you see. It'll be mentalist next.
RUBY	A nigger fag hillybilly sheister basket case towel-head. Hey – you got a full house.
DAVID	I'm a dartboard. A walking target. No one sees me. No one sees anyone anymore. You have no idea.
RUBY	Oh really? I have no idea. How may jews can you get in a Cadillac?
DAVID	What?

RUBY	Five hundred and four. Four in the seats and five hundred in the ash tray. Oh yeah. No idea.

(RUBY *crosses to* DAVID *and finds a photo in her purse.*)

RUBY	Take a look at this. My lot were German. Can you think of anything more ironic than a German Jew? That's the family. All sixteen of 'em. Never knew 'em but I paint my own picture. See the guy with the schnoz the size of a lemon? I figure he was a helluva of a hoot at a Bar Mitzvah, dancing on tables singin' like a foghorn. And look – those skinny gals with the round glasses and the contraceptive faces? Spinster cousins dreamin' of the day they get to break a glass and wear a ring. And the patriarch in the middle there. I reckon he was a professional. Dentist maybe. A mouth full of gold teeth and a wife who nagged him from dawn to dusk. Look at 'em all. Smiling. I reckon he must have cracked a funny. And the little girl at the front. With the curls. And the fat cheeks. The smile. That was my ma. My dear old ma. The only one who survived.

(RUBY *takes the photo back.*)

RUBY	I went there. To the camp. Few years ago. Took the tour. Saw the dormitories. The piles of glasses – those little round ones – the smashed up false teeth. The shoes. The rings. The ovens. And I walk out the gate which people only ever used to walk into and there's three kids. Young kids. Local kids. And they look at me. Work me out. And in their best English tell me the joke about the Cadillac . . . You gotta laugh. Eh?

(*A thumping at the door.*)

GEORGE	(*off*) OPEN UP. RUBY. RUBY. IT'S AN EMERGENCY. OPEN THE DOOR.

(DAVID *springs up, grabbing the gun.*)

DAVID
Someone's got to do something. Can't just roll over and let it happen.

BRIDIE ⎤
GEORGE ⎦
Open the door.
RUBY. RUBY.

RUBY
Then it was the Jews, sometimes it's the blacks, could be the friggin' Eskimos, but it's always someone. We all fight back and it's the end of the world. You gotta let it be.

DAVID
No. I won't let it be. I will not let it be. I REFUSE TO BE A VICTIM.

(GEORGE *manages to force the door and he and* BRIDIE *fall into the room.*)

GEORGE
Ruby, it's Jim...

BRIDIE
He's gone crazy in the classroom. Ripped up the picture of the Queen. She's leaving.

RUBY
He did what?

DAVID
Three people. (*Pointing the gun at* GEORGE, BRIDIE *and* RUBY *in turn.*) Person A. Person B and person C. Who's it to be? Who's it to be?

GEORGE ⎤
BRIDIE ⎬
RUBY ⎦
David. David. Please put the gun...
Oh God, no. DAVID.
Come on, kid, it's not...

(*The sound of the band in the distance playing 'Rule Britannia'. The Queen's legs, the corgis' legs and soldiers' legs appear on the podia as she prepares to leave the premises.*)

DAVID
Person A. A middle aged English father of a boy who's eating his way out of reality. Person B.

BRIDIE	David, please . . .
DAVID	An Irish woman deafened by her own biological clock. Or person C. An American capitalist with no guts.
RUBY	I got plenty, kid. Now put the . . .
DAVID	No . . . No . . .

(DAVID *waves the gun away from* GEORGE, BRIDIE *and* RUBY, *they assume he's going to aim for the Queen.*)

DAVID	I think it's got to be person D.

(DAVID *points the gun at his own head.*)

DAVID	A gay black Welshman with nothing left to lose.
GEORGE ⎤	NO.
BRIDIE ⎥	NO.
RUBY ⎦	NO.

(GEORGE *launches himself at* DAVID. *A shot is fired simultaneous to blackout. A corgi yelps.*)

Scene Two

The same. Two hours later – 4:30PM.

Police tape crosses the window, the gun display case and DAVID's *desk. A laptop with its lid open sits on the centre 'table'.*

ced JIM *sits, strangely static, smoking.* BRIDIE, *partially changed out of her national costume, stares blankly ahead, shocked, smoking.* GEORGE, *dishevelled, unbuttoned and bell-and-pig's-*

bladder-less with a cigarette hanging from his lips, strikes a match against the 'No Smoking' sign, lights his cigarette and takes the sign down from the wall. GEORGE *looks at his watch and hovers over the bell with his finger. He decides not to press it. All the teachers look like they've been through an emotional and physical war.*

A silence.

JIM   There's an Englishman, a . . .

                   (BRIDIE *and* GEORGE *look at* JIM. *He reconsiders and changes tack.*)

JIM   Have you heard about the . . .

                   (BRIDIE *and* GEORGE *again look at* JIM. *He has another try.*)

JIM   What's the difference between a . . .

                   (GEORGE *slams a book down on a surface, making* BRIDIE *jump.* JIM *recognises he is in new and dangerous territory. A silence. A sound indicates receipt of e-mail.* GEORGE *moves quickly towards the computer.* BRIDIE *and* JIM *make to move.* GEORGE *holds his hands up to keep them where they are. He opens the mail.* BRIDIE *and* JIM *watch him.*)

GEORGE   (*with difficulty*) With regard to the casualty . . . Low-calibre bullet. Blood loss . . . Severe trauma . . .

BRIDIE   Oh God.

GEORGE   With expert care and a long period of rest and convalescence . . . it is hoped that the corgi will live.

GEORGE ⎤   Oh, thank God.
JIM   ⎥   Phew.
BRIDIE ⎦   Yes.

RUBY	(*on PA*) ATTENTION. ATTENTION all group leaders and students. I would like to take this opportunity to apologise for any inconvenience this afternoon's shooting may have caused. Full cash refunds are available in reception. Please walk to the end of the drive for express coaches to Heathrow. Golf buggies are available for those still immobilised by shock. Thank you for staying at the United School of English. Do come see us again soon. (*Changing channels on the PA.*) George, Bridie Jim. What do you know? You turned a failing business into a bankrupt one. Stay put, schmucks. I wanna congratulate ya' in person.
	(*PA clicks off.*)
JIM	It's not our fault. It's David's fault. He's the one in the nut house.
GEORGE	You've got blood on your hands.
JIM	No. No, you cannae lay that at my door. I didn't squeeze the trigger. Sod him. He can go to straight to hell on a pit pony.
GEORGE	He's dying, Jim.
JIM	What?
GEORGE	Yes.
BRIDIE	Poor David.
JIM	No . . . No . . . Do you know what he did to me? Do you know what he . . . he touched me.
	(BRIDIE *checks the wall calendar.*)
BRIDIE	On this day in 1984 . . . AIDS was recognised. You've only had twenty one years to educate yourself.

JIM	Aye. Aye, but . . .
GEORGE	It isn't even HIV. That's right. Didn't think, did you? Didn't cross your mind for moment that it might be something else. Did it?
JIM	Everything's twisted. A minefield. I cannae help . . .
GEORGE	One last chance. To redeem yourself. Accept responsibility. Apologise.
JIM	He's not here you halfwit, he's gone. Finished.
GEORGE	To us. We're waiting.
BRIDIE	There's a human being in there somewhere. What are you so afraid of?

(*A silence.*)

JIM	I never . . . it's not balanced . . . It's one rule for the likes of him and one rule for . . .
GEORGE	There's the door.
JIM	WHERE'S MY JUSTICE? WHERE'S MY HUMAN RIGHTS? WHERE'S MY FREEDOM OF SPEECH?
BRIDIE	George.
GEORGE	Suspended. For the greater good. Go on. Get out. GET OUT. We're better off without you.

(JIM *explodes and sweeps a pile of books onto the floor.*)

JIM	Sassanachs be damned. Scotland rises. Caledonia is free.

(JIM *exits.*)

GEORGE	I'm a fool. A blind fool. A petty failure and a coward. Follow him, Bridie. Free yourself. This ship is sinking.

(BRIDIE *grabs* GEORGE, *turns him around and kisses him. A long kiss.*)

BRIDIE	You're a fair. Kind. Generous man.
GEORGE	I'm not.
BRIDIE	You are.
GEORGE	No, really. I'm not. Bridie, there's something you . . .

(*They kiss again.*)

GEORGE	Fire. Fire. I can see fire.
BRIDIE	Oh, me too. It's been a while.

(GEORGE *breaks from* BRIDIE *and heads to the window.*)

GEORGE	NO – out there. Jim. He's got the flag. Petrol. He's burning the union jack. The flagpost . . . Nelson's flagpost . . . (*Shouting off.*) NO. JIM. STOP.
BRIDIE	There's still Yankee soldiers out there. Christ, what is this? Baghdad?

(RUBY *enters in travel clothes with a bag.*)

RUBY	No. It ain't. I'm pullin' out. Hitchin' a lift with the marines. Nothing here for me now. I've had it with this tin-pot country.
BRIDIE	Oh great. That is just great.
GEORGE	Tin-pot. Tin-pot . . . HOW DARE YOU?

RUBY   I spoke to your Earl. He can have the joint back.

GEORGE   Have it back? Have it . . . You . . . you brought in the army. Decimated the lawns. Turned the long gallery into a casino and filled the lake with inflatable hamburgers.

(RUBY *looks out of the window.*)

RUBY   Looks like ya gonna have a fire in the west wing, too.

GEORGE   And you just want to hand it back?

BRIDIE   You can't just go. Not now.

GEORGE   You're leaving chaos in your wake.

RUBY   There's no money in ya. No money. No schmonney. What's a girl to do? But hey, I got some other projects in some other countries. So don't you go worrying about me.

GEORGE   Worrying about . . .

RUBY   (*off*) SPIN THOSE ROTORS, BOYS, I'M ON MY WAY. 'Course things might have been different. If I'd had the art and the baubles.

GEORGE   Baubles? Baubles? I'll give you baubles.

BRIDIE   Leave it. It's not worth it.

GEORGE   Not worth it. Not worth it, Bridie? It's worth everything. The fruits of thousands of years of history and knowledge and wisdom.

RUBY   You guys are so last century.

GEORGE   Our gifts to the world.

RUBY   BALONEY. What did you ever do for anyone else?

GEORGE	What? We – we – gave the world trade and communication.
RUBY	And slavery.
GEORGE	Cable under the ocean.
RUBY	Guns and disease. Oh, and opium, too.
GEORGE	Art and literature and culture from around the globe for our children.
RUBY	Keep it in the family.
GEORGE	Order. Civility. Justice . . .
RUBY	And I gave you a Coca-Cola machine. It's a fair trade.
GEORGE	AND TRUTH.

(*A silence. The blades on the helicopter on the lawn begin to turn.* RUBY *looks at* GEORGE. BRIDIE *looks at* GEORGE.)

RUBY	Oh, Truth? So now you wanna talk about truth?
GEORGE	Ah – I – Bridie. Fire extinguishers. In the games cupboard, could you . . .
RUBY	Oh no. The girl needs to know. Needs to know what she's got.
BRIDIE	What's she going on about, George?
GEORGE	It's . . . I . . .
RUBY	Wanna fess up, big guy? Shed some light? I worked it all out. I knew it had to be you.
GEORGE	I . . . I . . .
BRIDIE	What? What's he done?

GEORGE	I thought I was doing the right thing. I . . .
RUBY	So where'd you hide the treasure?
BRIDIE	George?
GEORGE	It was . . . I was . . . oh . . . oh . . .
RUBY	Come on. It's good for the soul. Or do the cops come back again? Your call.
GEORGE	Oh God. Alright. Alright.
BRIDIE	George?
RUBY	Lead the way. Where is it? Buried in the garden?

(GEORGE *realises he's cornered. He pulls a plant from a pot to reveal a medieval helmet.*)

GEORGE	Item one.
BRIDIE	That's a plant pot.
GEORGE	No. It's a medieval helmet. (*He puts it on his head.*) Blood stains still visible on the visor. From . . . Agincourt. Agincourt, Ruby.
RUBY	So what's Agincourt? A mall?
BRIDIE	What the . . .

(GEORGE *lifts the window pole and pulls off its outer sheath to reveal a long spear.*)

GEORGE	Item two. A long spear. The Wars of the Roses. Lancastrian versus York.
BRIDIE	Oh my God. George. What have you done?
RUBY	There's more. There must be a whole lot more.

	(GEORGE *opens up the inside of the photocopier.*)
GEORGE	Item three. Pewter goblets dating from 1066. The Battle of Hastings.
RUBY	Look at dat. You have been a very, very, naughty boy.
BRIDIE	That's why it wasn't workin'. George, how could you? You lied to me . . . God, be careful. What are you . . .
	(GEORGE *sweeps everything off the central table and overturns the flat surface – it is a huge canvas which he stands on it's end.*)
GEORGE	Item number four. The Stubbs.
RUBY	What do you know, it's the freaky horse.
BRIDIE	How in the hell did you keep all this secret?
GEORGE	Not to mention . . . .
	(GEORGE *turns over a series of cheap prints on the walls to reveal masterpieces.*)
GEORGE	A Whistler. A Turner and a Constable.
BRIDIE	Holy mother of God.
	(GEORGE *pulls artefacts from cupboard.*)
GEORGE	A Chippendale chair. A Clarice Cliff pot and last, but by no means least . . .
	(GEORGE *pokes at the ceiling with his pole bringing down the St. George's flag revealing a glass chandelier. He wraps the flag around himself. A fire alarm sounds in the distance.*)
RUBY ⎤ BRIDIE ⎦	Wow look at that. What the hell is that?

GEORGE	A Liberty chandelier circa 1927. Isn't it just . . . just exquisite. History. Craft – genius handed down through the ages. Cared for. Protected. Oh God, Ruby, I couldn't do it. Couldn't let you take the precious past from us and trade it like hotdogs on the market place. Don't you see? It had to be preserved. It was my duty. Whatever the cost. It had to be saved. Conserved. Don't you see? We have to keep some things the same. Forever.
BRIDIE	You sacrificed David.
GEORGE	For the greater good, Bridie. For the greater good. For the sake of our little nation here.
RUBY	Getting smaller by the minute. (*Looking out of the window.*) And hotter.
BRIDIE	If you knew it was George why didn't you say something?
RUBY	Jehaysus. I don't do internal politics. I want to keep my youthful glow. Take good care of the schmutter. The Earl's gonna need it when he gets back. I hear he's broke. He needs to sell.
GEORGE	What? WHAT?
RUBY	Ain't nobody can afford to be a museum no more, Georgie boy. The world ain't no display case. It's a shop. (*Off.*) FULL STEAM AHEAD, BOYS, RUBY'S COMIN' THROUGH. Adios. Sayonara. Arrivederci. It's been a hellava scream.

(RUBY *exits.* GEORGE *approaches* BRIDIE. *She moves away.*)

GEORGE	Bridie. Bridie. Say something. Please. Say anything.

BRIDIE	An Englishman, an Irishwoman, a Scotsman and a Welshman are trapped on a burning bridge. An American shouts up from the river bank. 'Too much weight. It's gonna collapse. One of you has to go. Jump into the river.' 'I do this for Wales,' says the Welshman and he jumps. 'Not enough,' says the American. 'You're too heavy.' 'I do this for the glory of Scotland,' says the Scotsman and he jumps. 'Still not enough,' says the American. 'One more.' 'I do this for the glory of Ireland,' says the Irishwoman. So she pushes the Englishman back into the fire. And then she jumps.
	(BRIDIE *exits.*)
GEORGE	NO. NO.
	(*The fire engine arrives. Blackout.*)